AGAINST THE RAGING SEA

STORIES FROM THE GOLDEN AGE

Edited by John Bell

Pottersfield Press, Lawrencetown Beach, Nova Scotia,
Canada

National Library of Canada Cataloguing in Publication

Main entry under title:

    Against the raging sea: stories from the golden age / John Bell, editor.

ISBN 1-895900-48-4

1. Sea stories, Canadian (English) — Atlantic Provinces. I. Bell, John, 1952-
PS8323.S4A32 2002   C813'.010832162 C2002-902849-3
PR9197.35.S43A32 2002

Cover image:
On the Deck of the Ship Torrens, by Jack Gray
Oil on canvas 91 x 152 cm.
Art Gallery of Nova Scotia
Reproduced with the permission of the Gray family.

Pottersfield Press acknowledges the ongoing support of the Nova Scotia Department of Tourism and Culture, Cultural Affairs Division. We acknowledge the support of the Canada Council for the Arts which last year invested $19.1 million in writing and publishing throughout Canada. We also acknowledge the finanacial support of the Government of Canada through the Book Publishing Industry Development Program for our publishing activities.

Pottersfield Press
83 Leslie Road
East Lawrencetown, Nova Scotia, Canada B2Z 1P8
Web site: www.pottersfieldpress.com
To order, phone 1-800-NIMBUS9 (1-800-646-2879)
Printed in Canada

Canada Council for the Arts   Conseil des Arts du Canada   NOVA SCOTIA Tourism and Culture

For my grandsons,
Cameron Tyler Bell and Mason John Bell,
who are growing up as they should —
by the sea.

Contents

Introduction

*Considering the fact that the fisherfolk form
so small and isolated a factor in the Canadian population,
they have been unusually well interpreted in literature.*
— Lionel Stevenson, 1926

The sea story has figured prominently in the literature of Atlantic Canada. During the latter part of the nineteenth century, many of the region's leading authors turned to the writing of sea fiction, most of it intended for juvenile readers. Typical works of the era included James De Mille's *Lost in the Fog* (1870), Charles W. Hall's *Adrift in the Ice Fields* (1877), James Macdonald Oxley's *The Wreckers of Sable Island* (1894), B. Freeman Ashley's *Dick and Jack's Adventures on Sable Island* (1895), and Charles G.D. Roberts' *Reuben Dare's Shad Boat* (1895). This period also saw the maritime life of the Atlantic region portrayed in the work of foreign writers such as R.M. Ballantyne, Kirk Munroe, and Rudyard Kipling.

Furthermore, two particularly notable Atlantic authors of sea-related non-fiction were active during this same era. Joshua Slocum, an expatriate Nova Scotian living in New England, and John Taylor Wood, a former Confederate States naval officer exiled in Halifax, both contributed important maritime memoirs to major American magazines. Slocum's third autobiographical narrative, *Sailing Alone Around the World* (1900), has long been recognized as one of the world's greatest classics of sea literature. Wood's exploits were even featured in Nova Scotia school readers and were later celebrated in *The Tallahassee* (1945), a long narrative poem by the Halifax poet Andrew Merkel.

The sea story has also formed an important current within modern Atlantic prose. Since the 1930s, many of the region's most prominent writers – including Thomas H. Raddall (who actually began publishing sea stories in the late twenties), Will R. Bird, Evelyn Richardson, Farley Mowat, Alistair MacLeod, Silver Donald Cameron, Antonine Maillet, and Lesley Choyce – have depicted the experiences of fishermen, sealers, rum-runners, and other mariners in fiction or non-fiction. At the same time, Atlantic Canada has continued to figure in the sea writing of authors from outside the region, such as the Canadian Victor Suthren; the Americans Edmund Gilligan, Marsden Hartley (who also painted Lunenburg County seafaring life), E. Annie Proulx, and Sebastian Junger; and the British writers Frank Knight and Patrick O'Brian.

The most significant era in the history of Atlantic Canadian maritime writing, though, was the period from 1900 to 1930. Not only was the region and/or its mariners depicted in works by Jack London, James Connolly, George Allan England, and other foreign writers, but, more importantly, these years saw many Atlantic authors draw inspiration from the seafaring traditions of the Maritimes and Newfoundland. The best Atlantic Canadian sea stories of the period were produced by ten writers: Wilfred T. Grenfell, Colin McKay, Norman Duncan, W. Albert Hickman, Theodore Goodridge Roberts, Frederick William Wallace, Archibald MacMechan, Arthur Hunt Chute, Erle R. Spencer, and Frank Parker Day. Their sea-related fiction and non-fiction represent an unjustly neglected chapter in regional literature: the golden age of the Atlantic sea story. It is this body of writing that is the focus of *Against the Raging Sea: Stories from the Golden Age.*

While these authors did not constitute a formal literary group, there were significant connections between many of them. Duncan, for instance, was initially sent to Newfoundland by *McClure's Magazine* to report on the good works of Dr. Grenfell. Grenfell, who later contributed forewords to two of Duncan's posthumous collections, also likely had contact with Spencer and Roberts. McKay was a contributor to Wallace's *The Canadian Fisherman*, and MacMechan corresponded with both Day and Wallace. Other links likely remain to be uncovered.

The three decades during which these writers, as a group, produced close to forty volumes of sea writing (not to mention dozens of uncollected magazine pieces) were a time of profound change in Atlantic Canada. The golden age of sail was becoming a memory, although many schooners continued to be built for both the fisheries and local and international coastal trade. In the Maritimes, these were years shaped by urbanization, modernization, industrialization, and progressive reform, including prohibition. Furthermore, the impact of these new social forces was heightened after the First World War by a severe economic depression, which led to a substantial exodus from the region, political and social unrest, and the strengthening of a regional consciousness that had begun to take shape at the turn of the century.

In the Maritime provinces, this regionalism was eventually manifested politically in the Maritime Rights movement, which sought to increase the region's influence within Confederation. Not surprisingly, regional sentiment also found strong expression in culture, much of it centring on the most crucial aspect of Atlantic Canada's identity – its relationship with the sea. It was, after all, an era when a fishing schooner, the *Bluenose*, came to serve as a potent symbol of regional pride following her victories in the 1921 and 1922 International Fishermen's Trophy races.

Although the writing of the sea-story authors represented one of the most important aspects of the seaward thrust of much Atlantic culture during the 1900-1930 era, other cultural producers were equally intent on recording the region's maritime experience. Among those active in this movement were the folklorists James Murphy, Gerald Doyle, Roy Mackenzie, and Helen Creighton; the narrative poets Robert Norwood (a leading member of the Halifax-based Song Fishermen poetry group) and E. J. Pratt; the artist Rockwell Kent (who lived in the Newfoundland outport of Brigus from February 1914 to July 1915); and the photographer Wallace R. MacAskill. As well, Atlantic seafaring life was portrayed in various films, including *The Doctor of Afternoon Arm* (1916), based on a short story by Duncan; *Blue Water* (1922) and *Captain Salvation* (1927), adapted from novels by Wallace; and *The Viking* (1931), which featured an on-screen appearance by Grenfell.

While the sea-story writers were encouraged by – and, in turn, helped to foster – the development of regional consciousness, their interest in fishermen and other seafarers can also be attributed, at least in part, to the dictates of the literary marketplace. From 1900 to 1930, there was an enormous demand for fiction. Not only did general-interest magazines in Canada, the United States, and Britain regularly publish short stories and serials, but there was also, in North America, a proliferation of pulp magazines (named for their cheap paper stock) devoted mostly to fiction. In addition to a growing market for fiction in general, there was a particular interest in stories featuring local colour or adventure. Especially successful were genres that combined both, such as the western and the northern-adventure story.

Between them, the sea-story writers appeared in most of the leading American, Canadian, and British periodicals of their day. To readers of *McClure's, Canadian Magazine, Maclean's*, and some of the other more staid magazines of the era, stories about fisherfolk living at the northeastern edge of North America made for exotic reading. To the readership of pulps such as *Adventure, Blue Book, Argosy*, and *Sea Stories*, the relative primitiveness of the region's maritime environment represented a perfect setting for the two-fisted heroism that they had come to expect in fiction. Of course, by the turn of the century, tales of the sea had become a mainstay of adventure fiction, as evidenced by Stephen Leacock's spoof of the genre in *Nonsense Novels* (1911).

The widely published Atlantic sea stories had much to recommend them: local colour, stirring drama and adventure, and the elemental struggle of man against the sea. It was a combination that was especially appealing for male readers. However, despite the strong elements of masculine adventure found in much of the work of the sea-story writers, their writing is not merely conventional adventure fiction. Nor is it primarily a nostalgic evocation of a lost golden age of wooden ships and iron men, which is how social historians have tended to characterize the work of several of the sea-story authors, especially the post-war writings of Mac-Mechan and Wallace.

While interest in the region's marine heritage did increase as Atlantic Canada's economic and social crisis deepened in the 1920s, a significant portion of the work of the Atlantic sea-story writers appeared in the more prosperous, forward-looking period that preceded the First World War. And even after the war, much of their writing dealt with what was for them contemporary seafaring life during the final decades of the age of sail.

For the most part, these writers – several of whom worked as journalists – were not given to lyrical explorations of the sea's eternal mysteries. Instead, the focus of the Atlantic sea story was mostly on the region's mariners and the quiet courage and fortitude which they displayed as they routinely pitted themselves against the sea's dangers. And while some of the sea-story writers obviously made concessions to the demands of the literary marketplace, they all strove for authenticity in their depiction of seafaring life. As a result, several are regarded as early realists. A key factor contributing to the accuracy and immediacy of the group's portrayal of maritime life was their ability to draw, to varying degrees, on first-hand experience.

Certainly in their day the Atlantic sea-story writers were viewed as sympathetic chroniclers of the authentic maritime culture of Atlantic Canada. Not only did editors, publishers, and the reading public respond favourably to their work, but so did contemporary critics. From 1920 to 1930, five major surveys of Canadian literature appeared. Between them, these works discussed most of the writers represented in *Against the Raging Sea*. The most sustained and perceptive examination of the Atlantic-Canadian sea story was found in Lionel Stevenson's *Appraisals of Canadian Literature* (1926), which included a chapter entitled "Down to the Sea in Ships." Stevenson dealt with five of the sea-story authors: Duncan, Wallace, Roberts, Grenfell, and MacMechan, attributing their success to both a commitment to authenticity and the "simplicity of the situation" encountered in their work.

In spite of the recognition that the sea-story writers eventually achieved, by the late 1920s the golden age of the Atlantic sea story was coming to an end. Grenfell was approaching the final years of his writing career. Duncan had by then died of a heart attack. McKay had stopped writing sea tales, and Hickman had given up literature for a successful marine business. Roberts was working mostly in other genres, while Wallace had turned to maritime history. In 1929, Chute was killed in a plane crash. Four years later, MacMechan died and Day was forced by ill health to retire.

By the time of Spencer's death in 1937, the sea-story writers were drifting into obscurity. Most of their *oeuvre* was out of print, a significant portion of it buried in difficult-to-obtain magazines. A variety of factors contributed to this neglect, including the rise of realism and modernism in Canadian literature and the increasing marginalization of regional culture.

This situation continued for several decades. The first sign of rediscovery came in 1968, when Malcolm Ross included Roberts' *The Harbor Master* in the New Canadian Library series. Three years later, Hickman's *Canadian Nights* was reissued in the United States. In 1973, Day's *Rockbound* finally appeared in its first Canadian edition, earning the praise of numerous critics, including George Woodcock, who admired the book for its depiction "of the harsh life of fishermen on the Atlantic coast, remarkably untrammeled by the stylistic affectations and moralistic fads that afflicted most Canadian fiction published before 1930."

Although only a small portion of the total output of the Atlantic sea-story writers has been republished, it is obvious that interest in at least some members of the group has gradually been increasing over the course of the past three decades. This renewed attention has coincided with the rebirth of Atlantic Canadian regionalism and the attendant growth of Atlantic studies. Today, researchers in various fields are attempting to recover the region's lost cultural heritage.

In 1995, I made my own small contribution to this process of literary salvage by editing the Pottersfield anthology *Atlantic Sea Stories*, the first book to examine these writers as a group (I am inclined to refer to them as the "Seaward School"). *Against the Raging Sea: Stories from the Golden Age* continues my explorations of Atlantic maritime writing from the 1900-1930 period. Most of the writers included in the original anthology are represented in this second volume; although, W. Albert Hickman, Erle R. Spencer, and Frank Parker Day, all of whom favoured the novel, are not included this time. (To compensate, Wallace and Chute are each represented by two stories.) As was the case with my first anthology, the selections are preceded by bio-bibliographical headnotes. I have also included some suggestions for further reading.

Both *Against the Raging Sea* and *Atlantic Sea Stories* grew out of my work as an archivist, more than two decades ago, at the Dalhousie University Archives, which holds the papers of such noted Atlantic writers of the sea as Archibald MacMechan, Frank Parker Day, and Thomas H. Raddall. Initially, I approached my sea-story research as a continuation of the historical and cultural work that I had begun during my early archival career; however, these maritime projects eventually took on a far more personal dimension, prompting me to reflect on my family's roots in Lunenburg County – especially the life of my grandfather, Charles S.A. Bell, a LaHave Islands fisherman who belonged to the world so vividly depicted in the tales of the golden-age authors. (In 1911, Charles Bell married Abbie Wolfe, whose grandfather, Henry, was apparently one of the survivors of the *Providence* disaster described in MacMechan's story "Via London," which is included in this volume.)

My grandfather died in 1955 – before he could share his seafaring experiences with me. The only keepsake that I have touching on his life at sea is his copy of the first edition of *Rockbound*. However, in the writings of Colin McKay, Frederick William Wallace, Arthur Hunt Chute, and the other regional sea-story writers, I have at last found an entry into his world. In the maritime reality evoked by these authors, I can stand, as Charlie Bell did, on the pitching deck of a Banks schooner, feel the biting wind and spray, and see, beyond the leeward rail, the dangerous splendour of the surging sea and above it the grey, looming sky. This is the real achievement of the Seaward School writers: with words they have preserved a world.

* * *

The compilation of *Against the Raging Sea* could not have been completed without the generous assistance of numerous people in Canada and the United States. I would particularly like to thank the staff of the National Library in Ottawa and the following individuals: Charles Armour, Richard Bleiler, Lesley Choyce, Mary Flagg, Anne Goddard, Donald M. Grant, Suzanne Hotte-Guibord, Lewis Jackson, Gary Kissal, John Leisner, John Locke, Harry Rennehan, Su Rogers, Ted Serrill, Brook Taylor, and Rena Van Dam.

John Bell
April 2002

Norman Duncan

Norman Duncan was born in North Norwich Township, Ontario in 1871 and grew up in Brantford and other Ontario communities. After spending four years at the University of Toronto, he became a journalist in the United States, first in Auburn, New York, and then in New York City. In 1900 *McClure's Magazine* sent him on the first of several trips to Newfoundland to document life in the outports. From 1901 to 1906 he taught at Washington and Jefferson College in Washington, Pennsylvania. In 1907, he moved to the University of Kansas. Although Duncan's later travels took him to the Middle East, Southeast Asia, and Australia, it was his time in Newfoundland that had the most lasting effect on his writing. Between 1903 and 1916 — the year of his death — he wrote numerous books about Newfoundland and Labrador, including *The Cruise of the Shining Light* (1907) and the Billy Topsail series of juvenile novels. Two more books, the sea-story collections *Battles Royal Down North* and *Harbor Tales Down North*, were published posthumously in 1918.

"The Fruits of Toil" first appeared in *McClure's Magazine* (July 1902) and was subsequently collected in *The Way of the Sea* (1903). Like all the stories in Duncan's first sea-fiction collection, it is written in the powerful documentary style that won him many admirers, including the noted British marine writer Frank T. Bullen, who observed "that with the exception of Mr. Joseph Conrad and Mr. Rudyard Kipling no writing about the sea has ever probed so deeply and so faithfully its mysteries as his. The bitter brine, the unappeasable savagery of snarling sea and black-fanged rock bite into the soul."

The Fruits of Toil

Now the wilderness, savage and remote, yields to the strength of men. A generation strips it of tree and rock, a generation tames it and tills it, a generation passes into the evening shadows as into rest in a garden, and thereafter the children of that place possess it in peace and plenty, through succeeding generations, without end, and shall to the end of the world. But the sea is tameless: as it was in the beginning, it is now, and shall ever be – mighty, savage, dread, infinitely treacherous and hateful, yielding only that which is wrested from it, snarling, raging, snatching lives, spoiling souls of their graces. The tiller of the soil sows in peace, and in a yellow, hazy peace he reaps; he passes his hand over a field, and, lo, in good season he gathers a harvest, for the earth rejoices to serve him. The deep is not thus subdued; the toiler of the sea – the Newfoundlander of the upper shore – is born to conflict, ceaseless and deadly, and, in the dawn of all the days, he puts forth anew to wage it, as his father did, and his father's father, and as his children must, and his children's children, to the last of them; nor from day to day can he foresee the issue, nor from season to season foretell the worth of the spoil, which is what chance allows. Thus laboriously, precariously, he slips through life: he follows hope through the toilsome years; and past summers are a black regret and bitterness to him, but summers to come are all rosy with new promise.

Long ago, when young Luke Dart, the Boot Bay trader, was ambitious for Shore patronage, he said to Solomon Stride, of Ragged Harbour, a punt fisherman: "Solomon, b'y, an you be willin', I'll trust you with twine for a cod-trap. An you trade with me, b'y, I'll trade with you, come good times or bad." Solomon was young and lusty, a mighty youth in bone and seasoned muscle, lunged like a blast furnace, courageous and finely sanguine. Said he: "An you trust me with twine for a trap, skipper, I'll deal fair by you, come good times or bad. I'll pay for un, skipper, with the first fish I cotches." Said Luke Dart: "When I trust, b'y, I trust. You pays for un when you can." It was a compact, so, at the end of the season, Solomon builded a cottage under the Man-o'-War, Broad Cove way, and married a maid of the place. In five months of that winter he made the trap, every net of it, leader and all, with his own hands, that he might know that the work was good, to the last knot and splice. In the spring, he put up the stage and the flake, and made the skiff; which done, he waited for a sign of fish. When the tempered days came, he hung the net on the horse, where it could be seen from the threshold of the cottage. In the evenings he sat with Priscilla on the bench at the door, and dreamed great dreams, while the red sun went down in the sea, and the shadows crept out of the wilderness.

"Woman, dear," said this young Solomon Stride, with a slap of his great thigh, "'twill be a gran' season for fish this year."

"Sure, b'y," said Priscilla, tenderly; " 'twill be a gran' season for fish."

"Ay," Solomon sighed, " 'twill that – this year."

The gloaming shadows gathered over the harbour water, and hung, sullenly, between the great rocks, rising all roundabout.

"'Tis handy t' three hundred an' fifty dollars I owes Luke Dart for the twine," mused Solomon.

"'Tis a hape o' money t' owe," said Priscilla.

"Hut!" growled Solomon, deep in his chest. "'Tis like nothin'."

"'Tis not much," said Priscilla, smiling, "when you has a trap."

Dusk and a clammy mist chased the glory from the hills; the rocks turned black, and a wind, black and cold, swept out of the wilderness and ran to sea.

"Us'll pay un all up this year," said Solomon. "Oh," he added, loftily, "'twill be easy. 'Tis t' be a gran' season!"

"Sure!" said she, echoing his confidence.

Night filled the cloudy heavens overhead. It drove the flush of pink in upon the sun, and, following fast and overwhelmingly, thrust the flaring red and gold over the rim of the sea; and it was dark.

"Us'll pay un for a trap, dear," chuckled Solomon, "an' have enough left over t' buy a — "

"Oh," she cried, with an ecstatic gasp, "a sewin' machane!"

"Iss," he roared. "Sure, girl!"

But, in the beginning of that season, when the first fish ran in for the caplin and the nets were set out, the ice was still hanging off shore, drifting vagrantly with the wind; and there came a gale in the night, springing from the northeast — a great, vicious wind, which gathered the ice in a pack and drove it swiftly in upon the land. Solomon Stride put off in a punt, in a sea tossing and white, to loose the trap from its moorings. Three times, while the pack swept nearer, crunching and horribly groaning, as though lashed to cruel speed by the gale, the wind beat him back through the tickle; and, upon the fourth essay, when his strength was breaking, the ice ran over the place where the trap was, and chased the punt into the harbour, frothing upon its flank. When, three days thereafter, a west wind carried the ice to sea, Solomon dragged the trap from the bottom. Great holes were bruised in the nets, head rope and span line were ground to pulp, the anchors were lost. Thirty-seven days and nights it took to make the nets whole again, and in that time the great spring run of cod passed by. So, in the next spring, Solomon was deeper in the debt of sympathetic Luke Dart — for the new twine and for the winter's food he had eaten; but, of an evening, when he sat on the bench with Priscilla, he looked through the gloaming shadows gathered over the harbour water and hanging between the great rocks, to the golden summer approaching, and dreamed gloriously of the fish he would catch in his trap.

"Priscilla, dear," said Solomon Stride, slapping his iron thigh, "they be a fine sign o' fish down the coast. 'Twill be a gran' season, I'm thinkin'."

"Sure, b'y," Priscilla agreed; "'twill be a gran' cotch o' fish you'll have this year."

Dusk and the mist touched the hills, and, in the dreamful silence, their glory faded; the rocks turned black, and the wind from the wilderness ruffled the water beyond the flake.

"Us'll pay Luke Dart this year, I tells you," said Solomon, like a boastful boy. "Us'll pay un twice over."

"'Twill be fine t' have the machane," said she, with shining eyes.

"An' the calico t' use un on," said he.

And so, while the night spread overhead, these two simple folk feasted upon all the sweets of life; and all that they desired they possessed, as fast as fancy could form wishes, just as though the bench were a bit of magic furniture, to bring dreams true – until the night, advancing, thrust the red and gold of the sunset clouds over the rim of the sea, and it was dark.

"Leave us goa in," said Priscilla.

"This year," said Solomon, rising, "I be goain' t' cotch three hundred quintals o' fish. Sure, I be – this year."

"'Twill be fine," said she.

It chanced in that year that the fish failed utterly; hence, in the winter following, Ragged Harbour fell upon days of distress; and three old women and one old man starved to death – and five children, of whom one was the infant son of Solomon Stride. Neither in that season, nor in any of the thirteen years coming after, did this man catch three hundred quintals of cod in his trap. In pure might of body – in plenitude and quality of strength – in the full, eager power of brawn – he was great as the men of any time, a towering glory to the whole race, here hidden; but he could not catch three hundred quintals of cod. In spirit – in patience, hope, courage, and the fine will for toil – he was great; but, good season or bad, he could not catch three hundred quintals of cod. He met night, cold, fog, wind, and the fury of waves, in their craft, in their swift assault, in their slow, crushing descent; but all the cod he could wrest from the sea, being given into the hands of Luke Dart, an honest man, yielded only sufficient provision for food and clothing for himself and Priscilla – only enough to keep their bodies warm and still the crying of their stomachs. Thus, while the nets of the trap rotted, and Solomon came near to middle age, the debt swung from seven hundred dollars to seven, and back to seventy-three, which it was on an evening in spring, when he sat with Priscilla on the sunken bench at the door, and dreamed great dreams, as he watched the shadows gather over the harbour water and sullenly hang between the great rocks, rising all roundabout.

"I wonder, b'y," said Priscilla, "if 'twill be a good season – this year."

"Oh, sure!" exclaimed Solomon. "Sure!"

"D'ye think it, b'y?" wistfully.

"Woman," said he, impressively, "us'll cotch a hape o' fish in the trap this year. They be millions o' fish t' the say," he went on excitedly; "millions o' fish t' the say. They be there, woman. 'Tis oan'y for us t' take un out. I be goain' t' wark hard this year."

"You be a great warker, Solomon," said she; "my, but you be!"

Priscilla smiled, and Solomon smiled; and it was as though all the labour and peril of the season were past, and the stage were full to the roof with salt cod. In the happiness of this dream they smiled again, and turned their eyes to the hills, from which the glory of purple and yellow was departing to make way for the misty dusk.

"Skipper Luke Dart says t' me," said Solomon, "that 'tis the luxuries that keeps folk poor."

Priscilla said nothing at all.

"They be nine dollars agin me in seven years for crame o' tarter," said Solomon. "Think o' that!"

"My," said she, "but 'tis a lot! But we be used to un now, Solomon, an' we can't get along without un."

"Sure," said he, "'tis good we're not poor like some folk."

Night drove the flush of pink in upon the sun and followed the red and gold of the horizon over the rim of the sea.

"'Tis growin' cold," said she.

"Leave us goa in," said he.

In thirty years after that time, Solomon Stride put to sea ten thousand times. Ten thousand times he passed through the tickle rocks to the free, heaving deep for salmon and cod, thereto compelled by the inland waste, which contributes nothing to the sustenance of the men of that coast. Hunger, lurking in the shadows of days to come, inexorably drove him into the chances of the conflict. Perforce he matched himself ten thousand times against the restless might of the sea, immeasurable and unrestrained, surviving the gamut of its moods because he was great in strength, fearlessness, and cunning. He weathered four hundred gales, from the grey gusts which come down between Quid Nunc and the Man-o'-War, leaping upon the fleet, to the summer tempests, swift and black, and the first blizzards of winter. He was wrecked off the Mull, off the Three Poor Sisters, on the Pancake Rock, and again off the Mull. Seven times he was swept to sea by the off-shore wind. Eighteen times he was frozen to the seat of his punt; and of these, eight times his feet were frozen, and thrice his festered right hand. All this he suffered, and more, of which I may set down six separate periods of starvation, in which thirty-eight men, women, and children died – all this, with all the toil, cold, despair, loneliness, hunger, peril, and disappointment thererin contained. And so he came down to old age – with a bent back, shrunken arms, and filmy eyes – old Solomon Stride, now prey for the young sea. But, of an evening in spring, he sat with Priscilla on the sunken bench at the door, and talked hopefully of the fish he would catch from his punt.

"Priscilla, dear," said he, rubbing his hand over his weazened thigh, "I be thinkin' us punt fishermen'll have a — "

Priscilla was not attending; she was looking into the shadows above the harbour water, dreaming deeply of a mystery of the Book, which had long puzzled her; so, in silence, Solomon, too, watched the shadows rise and sullenly hang between the great rocks.

"Solomon, b'y," she whispered, "I wonder what the seven thunders uttered."

"'Tis quare, that – what the seven thunders uttered," said Solomon. "My, woman, but 'tis!"

"'An' he set his right foot upon the sea,'" she repeated, staring over the greying water to the clouds which flamed gloriously at the edge of the world, " 'an' his left foot on the earth —' "

"'An' cried with a loud voice,'" said he, whispering in awe, "'as when a lion roareth; an' when he had cried, *seven thunders uttered their voices.*'"

"'Seven thunders uttered their voices.'" said she; "'an' when the seven thunders had uttered their voices, I was about to write, an' I heard a voice from heaven sayin' unto me, Seal up those things which the seven thunders uttered, an' write them not.'" [1]

The wind from the wilderness, cold and black, covered the hills with mist; the dusk fell, and the glory faded from the heights.

"Oh, Solomon," she said, clasping her hands, "I wonder what the seven thunders uttered! Think you, b'y, 'twas the kind o' sins that can't be forgiven?"

"'Tis the seven mysteries!"

"I wonder what they be," said she.

"Sh-h-h, dear," he said, patting her grey head; "thinkin' on they things'll capsize you an you don't look out."

The night had driven all the colour from the sky; it had descended upon the red and gold of the cloudy west, and covered them. It was cold and dark.

"'An' seven thunders uttered their voices,'" she said, dreamily.

"Sh-h-h, dear!" said he. "Leave us goa in."

---

[1] The Revelation of St. John the Divine, chap. x., 2-4.

Twenty-one years longer old Solomon Stride fished out of Ragged Harbour. He put to sea five thousand times more, weathered two hundred more gales, survived five more famines – all in the toil for salmon and cod. He was a punt fisherman again, was old Solomon; for the nets of the trap had rotted, had been renewed six times, strand by strand, and had rotted at last beyond repair. What with the weather he dared not pit his failing strength against, the return of fish to Luke Dart fell off from year to year; but, as Solomon said to Luke, "livin' expenses kep' up wonderful," notwithstanding.

"I be so used t' luxuries," he went on, running his hand through his long grey hair, "that 'twould be hard t' come down t' common livin'. Sure, 'tis sugar I wants t' me tea – not black-strap. 'Tis what I l'arned," he added, proudly, "when I were a trap fisherman."

"'Tis all right, Solomon," said Luke. "Many's the quintal o' fish you traded with me."

"Sure," Solomon chuckled; "'twould take a year t' count un."

In course of time it came to the end of Solomon's last season – those days of it when, as the folk of the coast say, the sea is hungry for lives – and the man was eighty-one years old, and the debt to Luke Dart had crept up to $230.80. The offshore wind, rising suddenly, with a blizzard in its train, caught him alone on the Grappling Hook grounds. He was old, very old – old and feeble and dull: the cold numbed him; the snow blinded him; the wind made sport of the strength of his arms. He was carried out to sea, rowing doggedly, thinking all the time that he was drawing near the harbour tickle; for it did not occur to him then that the last of eight hundred gales could be too great for him. He was carried out from the sea, where the strength of his youth had been spent, to the Deep, which had been a mystery to him all his days. That night he passed on a pan of ice, where he burned his boat, splinter by splinter, to keep warm. At dawn he lay down to die. The snow ceased, the wind changed; the ice was carried to Ragged Harbour. Eleazar Manuel spied the body of Solomon from the lookout, and put out and brought him in – revived him and took him home to Priscilla. Through the winter the old man doddered about the harbour, dying of consumption. When the tempered days came – the days of balmy sunshine and cold evening winds – he came quickly to the pass of glittering visions, which, for such as die of the lung trouble, come at the end of life.

In the spring, when the *Lucky Star*, three days out from Boot Bay, put into Ragged Harbour to trade for the first catch, old Skipper Luke Dart was aboard, making his last voyage to the Shore; for he was very old, and longed once more to see the rocks of all that coast before he made ready to die. When he came ashore, Eleazar Manuel told him that Solomon Stride lay dying at home; so the skipper went to the cottage under the Man-o'-War to say good-bye to his old customer and friend – and there found him, propped up in bed, staring at the sea.

"Skipper Luke," Solomon quavered, in deep excitement, "be you just come in, b'y?"

"Iss – but an hour gone."

"What be the big craft hangin' off shoare? Eh – what be she, b'y?"

29

There had been no craft in sight when the *Lucky Star* beat in. "Were she a fore-an'-after, Solomon?" said Luke, evasively.

"Sure, noa, b'y!" cried Solomon. "She were a square-rigged craft, with all sail set – a great, gran' craft – a quare craft, b'y – like she were made o' glass, canvas an' hull an' all; an' she had shinin' ropes, an' she were shinin' all over. Sure, they be a star t' the tip o' her bowsprit, b'y, an' a star t' the peak o' her mainmast – seven stars they be, in all. Oh, she were a gran' sight!"

"Hem-m!" said Luke, stroking his beard. "She've not come in yet."

"A gran' craft!" said Solomon.

"'Tis accordin'," said Luke, "t' whether you be sot on oak bottoms or glass ones."

"She were bound down north t' the Labrador," Solomon went on quickly, "an' when she made the Grapplin' Hook grounds she come about an' headed for the tickle, with her sails squared. Sure she ran right over the Pancake, b'y, like he weren't there at all, an' – How's the wind, b'y?"

"Dead off shore from the tickle."

Solomon stared at Luke. "She were comin' straight in agin the wind," he said, hoarsely. "Maybe, skipper," he went on, with a little laugh, "she do be the ship for souls. They be many things strong men knows nothin' about. What think you?"

"Ay – maybe; maybe she be."

"Maybe – maybe – she do be invisible t' mortal eyes. Maybe, skipper, you hasn't seed her; maybe 'tis that my eyes do be opened t' such sights. Maybe she've turned in – for me."

The men turned their faces to the window again, and gazed long and intently at the sea, which a storm cloud had turned black. Solomon dozed for a moment, and when he awoke, Luke Dart was still staring dreamily out to sea.

"Skipper Luke," said Solomon, with a smile as of one in an enviable situation, "'tis fine t' have nothin' agin you on the books when you comes t' die."

"Sure, b'y," said Luke, hesitating not at all, though he knew to a cent what was on the books against Solomon's name, "'tis fine t' be free o' debt."

"Ah," said Solomon, the smile broadening gloriously, "'tis fine, I tells you! 'Twas the three hundred quintal I cotched last season that paid un all up. 'Twas a gran' cotch – last year. Ah," he sighed, "'twas a gran' cotch o' fish."

"Iss – you be free o' debt now, b'y."

"What be the balance t' my credit, skipper? Sure I forget."

"Hem-m," the skipper coughed, pausing to form a guess which might be within Solomon's dream; then he ventured: "Fifty dollars?"

"Iss," said Solomon, "fifty an' moare, skipper. Sure you has forgot the eighty cents."

"Fifty-eighty," said the skipper, positively. "'Tis that. I call un t' mind now. 'Tis fifty-eighty – iss, sure. Did you get a receipt for un, Solomon?"

"I doan't mind me now."

"Um-m-m – well," said the skipper, "I'll send un t' the woman the night – an order on the *Lucky Star*."

"Fifty-eighty for the woman!" said Solomon. "'Twill kape her off the Gov'ment for three years, an she be savin'. 'Tis fine – that!"

When the skipper had gone, Priscilla crept in, and sat at the head of the bed, holding Solomon's hand; and they were silent for a long time, while the evening approached.

"I be goain' t' die the night, dear," said Solomon at last.

"Iss, b'y," she answered; "you be goain' t' die."

Solomon was feverish now; and, thereafter, when he talked, his utterance was thick and fast.

"'Tis not hard," said Solomon. "Sh-h-h," he whispered, as though about to impart a secret. "The ship that's hangin' off shoare, waitin' for me soul, do be a fine craft – with shinin' canvas an' ropes. Sh-h! She do be 'tother side o' Mad Mull now – waitin'."

Priscilla trembled, for Solomon had come to the time of visions – when the words of the dying are the words of prophets, and contain revelations. What of the utterings of the seven thunders?

"Sure the Lard he've blessed us, Priscilla," said Solomon, rational again. "Goodness an' marcy has followed us all the days o' our lives. Our cup runneth over."

"Praise the Lard," said Priscilla.

"Sure," Solomon went on, smiling like a little child, "we've had but eleven famines, an' we've had the means o' grace pretty reg'lar, which is what they hasn't t' Round 'Arbour. We've had one little baby for a little while. Iss – one de-ear little baby, Priscilla; an' there's them that's had none o' their own, at all. Sure we've had enough t' eat when they wasn't a famine – an' bakin' powder, an' raisins, an' all they things, an' sugar, an' rale good tea. An' you had a merino dress, an' I had a suit o' rale tweed – come straight from England. We hasn't seed a railroad train, dear, but we've seed a steamer, an' we've heard tell o' the quare things they be t' St. Johns. Ah, the Lard he've favoured us above our deserts: He've been good t' us, Priscilla. But, oh, you hasn't had the sewin' mach-ane, an' you hasn't had the peach-stone t' plant in the garden. 'Tis my fault, dear – 'tis not the Lard's. I should 'a' got you the peach-stone from St. Johns, you did want un so much – oh, so much! 'Tis that I be sorry for, now, dear; but 'tis all over, an' I can't help it. It wouldn't 'a' growed anyway, I know it wouldn't; but you thought it would, an' I wisht I'd got un for you."

"'Tis nothin', Solomon," she sobbed. "Sure, I was joakin' all the time. 'Twouldn't 'a' growed."

"Ah," he cried, radiant, "was you joakin'?"

"Sure," she said.

"We've not been poor, Priscilla," said he, continuing, "an' they be many folk that's poor. I be past me labour now," he went on, talking with rising effort, for it was at the sinking of the sun, "an' 'tis time for me t' die. 'Tis time – for I be past me labour."

Priscilla held his hand a long time after that – a long, silent time, in which the soul of the man struggled to release itself, until it was held but by a thread.

"Solomon!"

The old man seemed not to hear.

"Solomon, b'y!" she cried.

"Iss?" faintly.

She leaned over him to whisper in his ear, "Does you see the gates o' heaven?" she said. "Oh, does you?"

"Sure, dear; heaven do be — "

Solomon had not strength enough to complete the sentence.

"B'y! B'y!"

He opened his eyes and turned them to her face. There was the gleam of a tender smile in them.

"The seven thunders," she said. "The utterin's of the seven thunders – what was they, b'y?"

"'An' the seven thunders uttered their voices,'" he mumbled, "'an' —'"

She waited, rigid, listening, to hear the rest; but no words came to her ears.

"Does you hear me, b'y?" she said.

"'An' seven – thunders – uttered their voices,'" he gasped, "'an' the seven thunders – said – said — '"

The light failed; all the light and golden glory went out of the sky, for the first cloud of a tempest had curtained the sun.

"'An' said —'" she prompted.

"'An' uttered – an' said – an' said —'"

"Oh, what?" she moaned.

Now, in that night, when the body of old Solomon Stride, a worn-out hulk, aged and wrecked in the toil of the deep, fell into the hands of Death, the sea, like a lusty youth, raged furiously in those parts. The ribs of many schooners, slimy and rotten, and the white bones of men in the offshore depths, know of its strength in that hour – of its black, hard wrath, in gust and wave and breaker. Eternal in might and malignance is the sea! It groweth not old with the men who toil from its coasts. Generation upon the heels of generation, infinitely arising, go forth in hope against it, continuing for a space, and returning spent to the dust. They age and crumble and vanish, each in its turn, and the wretchedness of the first is the wretchedness of the last. Ay, the sea has measured the strength of the dust in old graves, and, in this day, contends with the sons of dust, whose sons will follow to the fight for an hundred generations, and thereafter, until harvests may be gathered from rocks. As it is written, the life of a man is a shadow, swiftly passing, and the days of his strength are less; but the sea shall endure in the might of youth to the wreck of the world.

Colin McKay

Colin McKay was born at Shelburne, Nova Scotia in 1876. The son of a respected shipbuilder, he followed the sea for nearly three decades, serving on sailing vessels and then steamships, including passenger liners and, during the First World War, the British hospital ship S.S. *St. George*. Between his stints at sea and after his retirement from seafaring, McKay worked as a journalist, writing for both mainstream newspapers and various labour and socialist publications. As a Canadian Press correspondent, he played a role in promoting the international schooner races between the U.S. and Canada. He also gained some recognition as a contributor of sea fiction and non-fiction to *McClure's, Ainslee's, Adventure*, and other periodicals. By the time of his death at Ottawa in 1939, however, his maritime writings were largely forgotten. In fact, his contribution to Atlantic literature was only recently rediscovered with the publication of the first collection of his sea stories, *Windjammers and Bluenose Sailors* (1993), edited by Lewis Jackson and Ian McKay. In 1996 Ian McKay edited a follow-up collection focussing on Colin McKay's lost non-fiction: *For a Working Class Culture in*

Canada: A Selection of Colin McKay's Writings on Sociology and Political Economy, 1897-1939.

"Scotty" was originally published in *McClure's Magazine* (November 1908) and was later collected in *Windjammers and Bluenose Sailors*. With considerable poignancy, the story explores the human cost of the passing of the age of sail by focussing on the personal torment of one master mariner. "Scotty" also displays the qualities that prompted the noted American editor S.S. McClure to praise McKay's "tremendous ability in writing of the sea." According to McKay, his highly regarded *McClure's* stories were "more or less founded on personal experiences."

Scotty

The brigantine, stripped to topsails, was running before a southerly gale, plunging exultantly through the racing surges, piling athwart her steering bows tumbling arches of crystal foam. The mate, an ancient sea-bear, bulky in oilskins, stood by the binnacle watching the heaving decks, the straining sails, with impassive countenance and steadfast old eyes. Presently he glanced astern where the heavens were banking up with bulging blue-black cloudmasses in titanic convulsions; then, shuffling athwart, he flung back the hood of the companion.

"Ho, captain, you'd better come up here."

A young man with an unwholesome and irritable aspect poked his head above the scuttle and looked around quizzically:

"What's the matter now?"

"Time to heave to, sir."

"Heave to – in this breeze!" snapped the skipper. "Get out! I cal'late to make Halifax to-day some time."

"You'll not do it, sir. It'll be blowing feather-white before long, and as thick as a feather-bed. The sooner you heave to, the better."

The captain's cadaverous countenance darkened with wrath, and his fishy eyes blinked furiously.

"I'm running this ship," he snarled in his nasal, nagging tones. "And I'm tired of hanging around out here. I've made Halifax in thick weather before this, and I can do it again."

"If you keep her going, you'll have her on a lee shore in a howling snowstorm, and maybe lose her, and all hands," responded the mate quietly.

"Oh, you're getting frightened of your precious life, are you?" snorted the skipper, baring his yellow fangs contemptuously. "And you're the man that sailed famous clippers – that made famous passages? You're an old fraud. . . . And you think you'll get this packet next trip, do you? Old Scotty, shrunken old Scotty, master of a ship! Not if I know it. You're too old and nervous to go to sea." And growling to himself, he dropped below, banging the scuttle behind him viciously.

The mate's old eyes blazed with murderous ferocity, and his vigorous old frame trembled violently with the vehemence of his rage. "I'll be the death of that fellow yet," he muttered savagely. "If he cheats me out of my last hope of obtaining another command, I'll . . . " Slowly the grim, weather-bitten countenance cleared. "Ah, the fellow isn't worth getting mad at – a coasting skipper and a squarehead to boot. The owner won't listen to him."

Suddenly he turned about and glanced at the man at the wheel – a stalwart young fellow, with features set in a grimace of torture, hurling the spokes back and forth with frenzied effort.

"Steering hard, Young?"

The man answered explosively, in a sort of petulant fury, as though his temper had been strung to the bursting point by the strain of his relentless labour: "She'll kill a man, sir. Why don't you take charge of her, and heave her to? The old man's drunk or crazy."

The mate blazed at him angrily, "Answer me civilly, and don't pass opinions"; then, turning away, he moved forward to the break of the poop and bawled out in a great deep-toned voice that boomed down the wind like the roll of a drum: "Lay aft here, Johnson, and lend a hand at the wheel."

The ship sped on, bounding with fierce, bodeful leaps over the roaring billows, plunging recklessly into the troughs. She reeled before it like a wild thing, kicking up her heels as though in defiance of the great gray-headed combers swarming after her like a pack of monstrous and ravening wolves. She tore on, quivering and groaning, and the old mate watched her with quiet eyes.

After a time the day darkened, and, borne upon the wings of the wind, a flurry of snow swept whirring over the sea. The captain came on deck and looked about him briskly.

"At the rate she's traveling now, we ought to sight land in a few hours," he shouted cheerily.

"We're more likely to pile on a shoal," answered the mate angrily. "We can't see two miles ahead now, and we won't be able to see anything soon. You'll put her ashore if you keep on, and, by God, if you do, I'll be the death of you."

The captain laughed with amused contempt.

"Oh, don't excite yourself, Scotty," he growled irritably. "The weather is goin' to clear presently. That bank astern is the last of it; the glass is going up." Then, with a sudden outward thrust of his shaven chin, and a furious blinking of his beady eyes, he added vehemently, "And don't you threaten me, you old coot. If it wasn't for your gray head, I'd smash your face."

"Oh, don't let that stop you," retorted the mate truculently. "I'll tell you again, if you run her ashore – if you cheat me out of a command – I'll kill you."

Suddenly a snow squall swooped down, black and appalling, out of the boiling sky, and burst upon them. The ship, shuddering violently from the impact of it, seemed to spring forward like a race-horse at the prick of a spur. With a wild, scooping motion, she leaped from sea to sea, plunging her bows into the bastions of the fleeing surges till she filled her foredecks from rail to rail. Soon the hard-driven craft, heavy with the weight of water upon her, was crashing into it like a sledgehammer, and deadening her way till she only evaded by a hair's-breadth the headlong swoop of the toppling combers charging after her. She burrowed into it till it seemed she would bang her brains out or wrack herself to pieces, but the captain held on – held on till a huge comber, overtaking the flying craft, flung its foaming crest viciously over the topsail, knocking his feet from under him and nearly sweeping him overboard. When he got up, he was unnerved – in a funk.

"Get the topsails off her, Scotty," he yelled excitedly.

"They'll blow off, as soon as we start the sheets," answered Scotty composedly. "And then she'll lose headway and be pooped for sure. You might as well bring her to now – the topsails'll go as soon as they shake."

"Get the topsails in, I say – and be quick about it."

The captain took the wheel, and the mate went forward with the men. But before they started a thing, both topsail yards carried away at the slings and went over the bows in pieces; and the fore-topsail, speared by a falling spar flogged instantly into rags.

"Look out, boys. She'll heave to, now," the mate roared. And he sprang into the fore-rigging, followed by the men.

The stripped ship jarred wildly to port, and a sea, catching her under the counter, flung her broadside to it – hove her nearly on her beam-ends in the trough. Next moment a whooping gray-head pounced upon her, breaking right over the whole length of her, burying her completely under an avalanche of foam. As she emerged from the flood, she swung head to the gale and lifted to the succeeding seas bravely. She was swept clean – deck-houses wrecked, bulwarks torn, boats gone – and the captain missing from the wheel. The mate slid to the deck bawling:

"Lay aft, boys, and get the trysail on her. Look alive, or she'll be falling off."

In a few minutes she had the trysail on her and lay with her head under her wing, breasting the seas buoyantly. The mate gazed into the smother to leeward at the disheveled crests of the tumbling surges – then he turned to the man who had taken the wheel.

"Well, I guess the captain went down quick. I never saw a sign of him after that sea piled over her."

"Yes, sir. S'pose he was stunned or killed. Brute of a sea. Thought the decks would be stove."

Old Scotty looked at the ship wallowing in the swell. He had a command again, given him by the sea, the good salt sea that he had loved so long, that had not forgotten him in his old age. Slowly his hard old face broke into a smile of grim satisfaction, and his sturdy old frame seemed to swell with pride. He was master of a ship again – not much of a ship – not much of a ship for "Old Stormy" of the *Petrel*, the master of the smartest clipper that flew the stars and bars in the epic days of the sailing ship – but still a ship. He would no longer have to bear the insolence and scorn of an ignorant and ill-natured squarehead – not for a while, anyway. "Serve the fool right, too," he muttered grimly. He was a vindictive old man.

After a while he went down into the after cabin, and, standing in water to his knees, began to work over a chart spread on the table. Presently he straightened up with a savage imprecation: "Curse the fool! We'll be ashore if it don't clear off soon." He looked around – and saw a haggard and bloody face peering at him dazedly from under the raised curtain of the captain's berth. Old Scotty had seen too many of the wonders of the deep, of the mysteries of life, not to be superstitious; but it was characteristic of him that he gave no sign of being startled – didn't even start back. In the dim and unsteady light he gazed unflinchingly at this amazing apparition – and became aware that it was the captain himself, and in the flesh, too. When that sea broke over her, the old man had, by some freak of the swirling waters, been hurled head foremost down the companion and left with just enough life and sense to crawl into his bunk.

"You here?" said Scotty at length. "I thought you were overboard."

"Well, I'm not," snapped the captain. "How long have I been down here?"

"Not very long. Are you hurt?"

"My head's spinning like a top – that's all," growled the captain savagely. "Send the steward here, and get out of my cabin. You can't take charge of my ship yet a while."

"I wish to God I'd taken charge of her four hours ago, and saved the sea the trouble of breaking your head," cried Scotty passionately. "She's nearer land than I thought. If you're so smart, you'd better come up, and take her in . . . "

"Breakers – breakers under our lee!" came the startling cry from the deck. "Jump up here, sir. We're going ashore."

Scotty sprang on deck, and the skipper, who had apparently been more frightened than hurt, followed at his heels. The ship was pitching heavily in a smother of snow, in a storm of spray; and all hands were gathered aft gazing into the gloom to leeward. Soon a big comber, rushing in, broke with an ominous roar hardly a cable's length to leeward into a mighty mass of seething foam.

"Get the foresail on her," roared Scotty.

But before they reached the break of the poop, she struck with a shock that threw all hands to their knees. Next moment she was caught up by a giant roller and hurled stern foremost upon the reef, bringing up with another terrific jolt. All hands scrambled into the main rigging.

The ship lay in a welter of broken water, with her stern high on the shoal and her bows buried in the seas, thumping, shuddering, worried cruelly by the frenzied wash of the waves. Every comber, as it came whooping in, broke roaring over her sunken bows and rushed in an avalanche of foam over her poop.

The captain was crying like a child. "Oh, Scotty, what can we do?" he cries despairingly.

"Don't you Scotty me, curse you," roared the mate furiously. "You've got us in a nice fix, haven't you, with your pigheaded foolishness? You may as well say your prayers if you know any — you'll never get out of her."

The captain stopped blubbering and watched the ponderous rollers crashing over the hull beneath him. A man began to curse him bitterly. "Shut up," roared Scotty angrily. "I can do all the cursing necessary." And in his big voice, vibrating with the virulence of his rage, he proceeded to curse the captain, violently, vindictively. But the captain, watching the breaking seas, didn't seem to hear.

In a little while the weather cleared very suddenly, and they saw where they were. On either hand ragged ranges of breakers stretched away for miles, but to leeward, scarcely a mile distant, lay the land — treeless, snow-clad slopes, dotted with dreary-looking fishing huts. As they gazed, the gale dropped abruptly — died out completely; and soon black figures appeared on the white hills, and a big boat pushed out of a little cove and came bouncing off toward them over the short, easy seas inside the ragged line of breakers. At length it arrived under the lee of the shoal, a hundred yards away, and a man in the stern sheets began to gesticulate wildly with both arms, as though inviting the shipwrecked mariners to swim through the rollers raging furiously over the shoal.

"They might as well have stopped ashore," growled the captain savagely. "They haven't any rocket apparatus — the fools! Do they expect us to swim through the surf?"

Old Scotty looked at the drawn face of the captain, the dejected figures of the men, and smiled sardonically. He hated the lot of them – those chaps that called themselves sailors and hadn't sense or spunk enough to save themselves. He wouldn't lift a little finger to save any of them. And for himself he didn't care.

He had nothing to live for now – and memories of his redoubtable youth rose up suddenly and seemed to mock him. "Old Stormy" – he remembered how the rollicking clipper sailors used to sing of his sailcracking exploits in their wild chanteys – "Old Stormy" had been a man of mark; a man who had sailed famous ships, who had made records on all the deep-water routes. But the man he was had been dead these many years. "Old Scotty," drunken "Old Scotty," as a degenerate generation of seamen called him, was only an old derelict adrift upon the sea – of no more account in the modern scheme of things than a fleck of foam upon a broken wave. If he – the man who as master of the *Petrel* wrested the blue ribbon of the seas from the famous English clipper *Star of the East* – went to an owner now with his hat in his hand, he could not get a ship; he would probably be laughed at – told that the man he claimed to be had been dead and buried years ago. Suddenly – and for the first time in his dissolute old age – he felt he had made a mess of life, and a malignant fury of resentment seized him – a desperate and murderous rage against the captain, the men, fate, life, and all the changed facts of life. As in a revealing flash of lightning, he saw the wreck of his life, and his lost soul, baffled and humiliated, became the prey of a mad impulse to give his passion reign – to fling himself upon the captain, upon the men, and end it all in an orgy of violence, in a frenzy of ferocity.

"What can we do, sir?" queried a man despairingly.

Old Scotty looked at him, noticed the appeal in his strained eyes, and suddenly, with a sharply drawn breath, recovered his grip upon himself. Surely he was going mad – what was he thinking about? If the captain didn't know his duty, he did, and he was mate – with some responsibility for the lives of the men. What was he thinking of? They had never harmed him. It was his duty to see them safely out of the ship. But the captain – the man whose foolhardy pigheadedness had robbed him of his last chance of a command – should not escape. No, not if he had to kill him with his own hands. And for himself he did not care.

"We'll have to send a line down to them boys," he said quietly.

In a moment he dropped to the deck, and, though the waves were over him every few seconds, managed to make his way aft, secure a life-buoy and log-line, and return to the rigging again. Presently he tossed the buoy overboard, with the line attached, and slowly but surely it was carried by the rollers across the shoal.

The boat picked it up, dropped an anchor, and signaled to haul back on the line. They hauled until they got a tailed block with an endless fall wove through it; and when it had been made fast, a breeches-buoy was pulled off to them.

But none of the men cared to go in it. They looked at the giant combers roaring over the shoal, and were filled with dismay. Now and then, as the great billow broke with thunderous tumult, they caught glimpses of rocks, jagged, black, very vicious-looking, in the seething foam. They protested frantically that they wouldn't go – that they would be drowned in the surf – dashed to pieces upon the rocks.

Scotty turned to the nearest man. "Here you, get into it," he ordered fiercely. "Get into it, and none of your nonsense. You can't stop here, and there's no time to lose. She'll break up, or slide off the reef presently."

Suddenly the man laughed. "Well, here goes," he shouted. And, his face shining with a sort of desperate recklessness, he clambered into the buoy. Next moment he was in the surf, and the men in the boat were hauling away with a will. They saw him at intervals, high on a curling crest – saw him once gravely turning a somersault in the air – and finally saw him being lifted into the boat, whether alive or dead they could not tell. But the buoy was promptly hauled off again, and another man got into it and started on the dangerous journey through the jaws of death.

As the men were being hauled through the surf, the ship began to break up – break in two under the terrific blows of the billows crashing upon her sunken bows. Ere long the foremast fell without warning, nearly jerking the mainmast out of her, nearly slathing the men out of the rigging into the raging maw of the sea. And at last, as the second mate was leaving, the decks suddenly burst amidships, and the foreward part of the hull disappeared under a welter of foam.

Old Scotty looked at the captain clinging to the swaying, shaking rigging, and his grim face assumed an expression of unrestrained and gloating ferocity. The captain should not escape. When the buoy came off again, he would go in it, but while in the surf he would cut the line behind him.

"Well, you Dutch fool, you'll not get out of her – you'll not escape," he said in slow, venomous tones.

The captain's face was as white as a sheet, but his expression was essentially composed, as though he were resigned to death.

"I'm afraid not," he answered quietly. "I'm afraid the main-mast will go before it comes my turn. And I dare say it serves me right," he added hastily, in his old nagging, spiteful tones. "But it's hard – hard to leave a wife and children. God knows what will become of them. They had only my earnings to depend on."

Scotty looked at him curiously. Presently the hard old face softened, and the ferocious glitter died out of his eyes. The Dutchman had his faults, but after all they were more of head than the heart. And he had a wife and children.

"Captain, you'll go next," said Scotty dully.

The captain did not even look at him. "Oh, no – I'll wait my turn," he said wearily. "I'll pay the price of my folly, if need be."

Scotty watched the buoy skipping off towards them, and when it arrived he said again:

"Captain, you'll go next. Go to your wife and children. If I'm lost, it won't matter. There's nobody to miss me."

"No, no. I can't, man. I may be a fool, but I've some self-respect. And if you . . ."

Suddenly Scotty whipped out his sheath-knife, and, though at risk of being slathed into the sea, flourished it in the captain's face.

"Go, you fool, go, or I'll kill you," he cried in a fury. "Go to your wife and children before it's too late. If I don't get out of here, you can say you were hurt. Go, go – before I kill you."

The spar began to totter drunkenly, and the captain, bursting into tears, scrambled hastily into the buoy, and in a moment was sliding into the surf. Old Scotty, left alone in his rocking engine, laughed a strange, mocking laugh, as though in scorn of his weakness, as though in contempt of the relenting mood that made him forego his revenge. "And I'm a fool, too, I'm thinking," he muttered grimly, "throwing away my chance of life for a . . . Dutchman. Ah, well, I've lived my life – I've had my fling" . . . The mast suddenly seemed to spring up, the rigging parted, and spar and man plunged headlong into the sea. In a moment Scotty rose to the surface uninjured, and, all the combativeness of his indomitable old soul aroused by the shock of the icy waters, scrambled back upon the heaving spar and began to throw off his boots and clothes. Soon he noticed that the whip was jammed, and as the spar reared on a swell he saw that the captain was still in the surf. Instantly he flung himself into the water, caught hold of the hauling part, and, getting out his knife, cut the line behind him. As the whip gave to the strain upon it, he was jerked under, but he held on doggedly and was drawn into the surf, where the great combers picked him up and flung him, as though he were a ship, far forward, or buried him deep under a mass of foam, rolling him over and over like a waterwheel. Now and then he was dashed furiously upon the rocks, but he held on the line desperately. At last the roaring combers flung him, as though in disdain of his gray hairs, into smoother water, and he was hauled, breathless and dazed, into the boat by amazed and excited men.

"Good Lord! It's old Neptune himself," exclaimed the big, brown-headed coxswain.

Old Scotty lay full length in the stern sheets, puffing and blowing like a porpoise. Presently he gasped:

"ALL hands safe?"

"The captain's dead, six killed in the surf," answered the second. "But the rest of us are alive enough, though broken up a bit.

Guess we'll pull through – if we don't freeze to death before we get ashore."

Old Scotty, lying there too exhausted to move, groaned heavily. And so he had killed the captain after all – driven him to a dishonourable death.

"Ah, well," he muttered aloud, "the sea will have its way. But the captain was hurt before he left the wreck."

Frederick William Wallace

Born in Glasgow, Scotland in 1886, Frederick William Wallace moved to Canada with his parents in 1904. After working for shipping firms for several years, he became a freelance marine writer, illustrator, and photographer. In 1913 he founded *The Canadian Fisherman* and two years later helped to organize the Canadian Fisheries Association, serving as the organization's secretary until 1922. During the First World War he was the sailing master and navigator of a naval "Q" ship before taking charge of the Fish Section of the Canada Food Board. After working in the U.S. fishing industry from 1922 to 1928, he returned to Canada and co-founded National Business Publications Ltd. He also later rejoined the Canadian Fisheries Association. Apart from his work as a fisheries specialist, he was active as a writer of sea fiction and as a maritime historian. Among his many books were the novels *Blue Water* (1907) and *Captain Salvation* (1925), which were both made into movies; the story collections *The Shack Locker* (1916) and *Salt Seas and Sailormen* (1925); and the historical works

Wooden Ships and Iron Men (1924), *In the Wake of the Wind Ships* (1927), and *Record of Canadian Shipping* (1929). Wallace died in 1958. For a useful examination of his career, see M. Brook Taylor's article "Frederick William Wallace: The Making of an Iron Man" in the *Royal Nova Scotia Historical Society Journal* (Volume 4, 2001).

Wallace is represented here by two stories. The first, "Winter Fishing," originally appeared in *Adventure Magazine* (March 1913) and was subsequently reprinted in the collection *The Shack Locker.* One of several stories featuring Captain Harry Winslow that Wallace contributed to *Adventure,* "Winter Fishing" illustrates the degree to which even the most extreme hazards of seafaring had become almost commonplace for many of the fishermen of Atlantic Canada.

The second story, "Like a Proper Sailorman!," is taken from Wallace's *Salt Seas and Sailormen.* While much of Wallace's fiction celebrates the often extraordinary exploi of iron men, this tale is concerned with the desperate courage of a broken sailor barely clinging to his life at sea.

Winter Fishing

Winslow glared under sullen brows at the lowering sky and turned aggressively to Jimmy Thomas, who was hanging on to his dory-painter at the main rigging.

"I kin see it's dirty-looking, but I'll make a day of it in spite of th' weather —"

"Waal, Fred Hanson has his dories all aboard, Harry," answered the old fisherman, "an' ye can't take chances with th' weather on Brown's in th' month o' January. Th' glass has been a-tumblin' all day —"

"I don't care ef it has or not," growled the skipper. "I've got the chance to git a deck o' fish to-day an' I'm a-goin' t' git it. We've been lying-to for nigh six days now, an' 'tis about time we got a trip —"

"Ef ye'll take my advice, ye'll make this th' last set," persisted Thomas. "There's a south-easter amakin' up an' it'll come on quick an' sudden."

Winslow was in an ill humor. He considered that the elements were thwarting him in his efforts to make a successful trip, and Jimmy Thomas's advice was unfavorably received.

"I'll be hanged ef I ever knew sich an old croaker as you, Jimmy. 'Tis a regular Foul Weather Jack you're becomin', an' I wish ye'd mind yer own business. I'll look after th' weather – you look after th' fishin'."

Thomas looked at the skipper sharply. "Don't talk like a fool, Harry," he said bluntly. "Ye know what has happened in th' past by fellows riskin' th' weather an' runnin' chances. If *you* don't, I do; an' ye don't want t' listen to anythin' I say, it seems —"

This was too much for Winslow's pride and he resented the old fisherman's manner of speaking.

"You've got too dam' much t' say aroun' here, an' I don't want your advice. Keep on fishin' until I tell ye t' knock off or else stay aboard. When I want yer advice I'll ask ye for it; so git yer bait an' clear out."

Thomas's dorymate, Will Jackson, clambered out of the hold with a bucket of bait, as the skipper strode angrily away to the wheel, and he placed the bucket down and stared calmly at the rising swell and ragged stormy sky.

It was becoming dark already and the sunless January day was drawing to a close. The gulls, those ever-present trailers of the Bank fishermen in winter, had mysteriously disappeared, and Jimmy Thomas glanced apprehensively to leeward, while the skipper, at the wheel, glared at him resentfully.

"What'll we do Jimmy?" queried Will Jackson, ignoring the skipper's savage glances.

"Git th' torches an' jump in," answered the old man. "We'll make th' set."

Shipping the oars, they pulled away into the gathering darkness.

Five tubs had been set and hauled by each dory that day and, in the light of the torches, the crews ranged alongside the schooner and pitched out their fish in a swell which called for unusual dexterity on the part of the dory-mates.

Winslow was happy. He had wrested a huge fare from the waters of the Bank and there was a gladsome light in his eyes as he took in the over-flowing pens and fish-littered decks.

"Great work, boys," he said, as the last dory came up on the tackles. "Git yer suppers now an' start in dressing down. There's dirty weather ahead of us an' a thunderin' lot o' work t' do. All dories aboard?"

"All but Will Jackson an' Jimmy Thomas," answered a man.

Winslow started.

"By th' Great Trawl Hook! I clean forgot him. What tub is he on? Fifth?"

"No, skipper. He's settin' his sixth now. Jest went down as we was a-comin' in."

"Sixth?" ejaculated the skipper. "Why I thought he was only on his fifth! What in th' hell did that ol' fool want t' make another set for?"

"You told him, skipper," remarked a man pitching fish in the after-pen.

"Yes, I know I did," replied Winslow petulantly. "I was kinder riled this afternoon. Logan! Lay aloft an' see ef ye kin locate him.

I cal'late he's somewhere t' wind'ward. Thunderation! It's gettin' thick to th' s'uth'ard. D'ye see anything?"

"Nawthin' but another vessel dressing down!"

Jumping below into the cabin, the skipper pulled a pair of binoculars from under his bunk mattress and threw a hasty glance at the barometer. The sight caused him to pause and scrutinize the instrument with evident perturbation.

"Twenty-nine two!" he muttered. "Holy Sailor! She's tumbling – an' one dory still out. Hell!"

There was a half-breathed prayer on his lips as he jumped for the companion and scoured the darkening sea. Far to leeward the glare of torches marked a vessel cleaning her catch, but not a sign could he see of the lone torch-flare betokening a dory engaged in making a night-set.

"Sight anything?" he bawled to Logan at the masthead.

"Nawthin'," came the answer from the darkness aloft.

"Stand by for about! Git th' horn goin' some one! Knock off now, everybody, an' keep alook-out for that dory. Th' fish? Dam' th' fish! Thomas an' Jackson are out there somewheres an' it's a-goin' t' blow like hell soon!"

Winslow's voice almost rose to a shriek as he uttered the final words. The storm was coming. He could sense it in the rising lift of the sea, in the clammy chilliness of the breeze coming out of the southeast; and the young skipper's heart was encircled with the cold grip of fear.

It's not a nice thing to get men astray on the Banks in winter, and his imagination pictured the stubborn old fisherman and his dorymate out there in the darkness, tossing and heaving on the rising sea. And he, in his thoughtlessness, had sent them out! Sent them out in the wintery darkness with a southeaster close aboard, and all because he was too ill-natured to take advice from an old and true shipmate. As he tugged at the wheel of the reeling schooner, his heart was being flayed by the whip-lash of conscience.

A damp puff of air smote him in the face and, in the light which streamed from the binnacle and cabin-skylight, he could see that snow was commencing to fall. The sea and sky to leeward appeared as one solid wall, dense, opaque and heavy with ominous portent. Some one shouted, and the light of the vessels to leeward disappeared as though a mighty hand had snuffed them out.

Down came the squall. Logan's hail of its advance was dashed back in his teeth and the schooner, under three whole lowers, rolled down to the blast, while the air was filled with flying sleet and the whirring drone of the wind.

The fish piling the decks slithered like an oily wave over the lee rail and the crew staggered, slipped and tripped in the slimy mass as they jumped for rigging and weather-rail.

Winslow, with his mind brought back to present exigencies, ground the wheel over with a super-human effort until the vessel came to the wind and amid the thunderous rattle and bang of gear, his voice was heard in a steady, iron-lunged roar.

"Down with th' mains'l! All hands aft here!"

The huge seventy-five-foot boom was fetching up on the slackened tackles with nerve-rending shocks, and in the inky blackness the men raced aft to subdue the demon with fists, profanity and rude remarks. The heavy main-sheet blocks swayed and thumped to the jerks of the thrashing boom, and aloft in the awe-inspiring gloom the huge mainsail flapped in thunderous reports.

"Main-sheet!" roared Winslow above the din. "Bring her aboard! Git th' crotch shipped. Ready with your tackles! Slack up your boom-lift! Lower away easy! Steady on th' downhaul! Tie her up! All fast? Take th' wheel, Henderson. Heave her to on th' starb'd tack – I'm going below.

With a sympathetic "All right, Harry," the fisherman grasped the spokes. He knew what the young skipper's thoughts were, and Winslow, as he lay in his bunk, oblivious to the low whispers of the men coming below and the howl of the gale outside, passed through the hell of conscience for a bitter hour.

They were gone! Two of the men who had followed him trip after trip since he started as skipper. One of them had been his dorymate in the old days; and now he had repaid their devotion by sending them to their death on the chill, dark waters of the Bank.

II.

When he left the vessel after his tiff with the skipper, Jimmy Thomas and his dorymate pulled silently to windward. In silence they hove out the sling-ding and prepared to set the baited trawl.

Jackson was the first to speak.

"Th' skipper's beginnin' t' git like all th' rest of them. After they git a vessel an' make a few high-line trips, they know everythin' an' ye can't tell 'em nawthin'. He'll be as big a swab as Fred Hanson afore he's a year older."

Old Jimmy finished heaving out the trawl and, making the buoy fast to the dory, pulled out his pipe and lit up.

"You're wrong, Bill," said the old man calmly. "Harry Winslow 'll never be a man of th' Fred Hanson type, for he's a good lad an' allus will be. He was a bit hasty in his talk maybe, but he's young an' anxious t' make a trip after sich a poor winter. He's a young man to go as skipper, an' skippers hev a lot o' worries we common ornery trawl-haulers ain't got. So ye'll hev t' excuse th' lad his little bit o' jaw."

Jackson was an easy-going man with a child-like faith in his older dorymate and like a child he coincided readily with a stronger mind.

"I cal'late you're right, Jimmy," he said. "Let's haul now an' git aboard. 'Tis dirty-lookin' to th' s'uth'ard thar'."

With a torch flaring on the dory-gunwale the two proceeded to haul the gear. A few fathoms had scarce come in over the roller when the dory side-wiped a sharp, short comber which extinguished the torch, and, while Jackson was endeavoring to relight it again, the squall hit in. The trawl-line, which, for the time being, had been hitched around the heaving-stick stuck into a thole, parted as the dory rose on a sea, and they were adrift in the howling darkness.

As quick as thought, Thomas hove the dory anchor over and paid out the roding to the end.

"Five shot o' new gear gone," he cried to his dorymate, who was plying the oars and nursing the rearing dory over the hissing combers. "I cal'late we'll hang on till this blows past. Whew, ain't it a blinder? Blowin' an' snowin' an' black as the inside o' a jackboot. See any sign o' th' vessel, Bill?"

"I kin see nawthin'," panted Jackson.

Both men were aware of their danger, though neither voiced his fears.

Astray on the Bank with a gale of wind blowing, on a dark midwinter night, is a situation few fishermen ever care to be in, or even think about, and an eighteen-foot dory is a pitifully frail craft to brave the rage of a North Atlantic winter on open water. Trusting to the slender twenty-four-pound line to hold them to their position, the two fishermen laid to their oars and manoeuvred the dory among the huge seas that were now rising to the lash of the wind.

"We'll hang on here as long as the anchor will. Winslow 'll beat up to us an' it's better t' keep yer position than t' let go an' wander all over th' Bank a-lookin' for th' vessel. Let th' vessel look for us. Can't git that torch alight, ye say? Wet, is it? That's bad. It'll give Winslow no chance t' make out where we are — Thunder an' blazes! The blame anchor's parted. Head her up to it or we'll be over!"

Shying and cavorting like an untamed broncho, the dory started to whirl down to leeward and, though it was snowing heavily and bitterly cold, the two men perspired with their exertions as they tugged with short strokes at the oars. Thomas punctuated his efforts with occasional bursts of lurid profanity, with a reckless disregard to the probability of his precipitation into Eternity at a moment's notice, and his dorymate worried over the fact that he was hungry.

"Ain't no sign o' th' vessel, Will. I cal'late we're agoin' t' spend th' whole blank night out here, an' that ain't what I'm hankerin' after."

Jackson grunted assent. "Gee!" he said, "Wouldn't I jest like t' be muggin'-up now, Jimmy. An' th' cook was amakin' doughnuts an' lemon pies fur supper!" Jackson's mouth watered at the thought. "Say, Jimmy," he added, "that squall ain't easin' off any. There's th' very hell of a sea runnin' now an' it's snowin' thicker'n ever."

"Aye," answered the other. "She's black an' dirty to-night, fo' sure. Give us a chew, Will."

Hour after hour went by and still they reeled and whirled about on the wind-harried waters. Moments there were when a creaming crest threatened to overwhelm them, but a skilful lunge of the oars sent the little boat mounting the menace without shipping a bucketful of water. It was hard, nerve-straining work – a veritable game with Death – and, as the minutes went by with no sign of a vessel, both men knew that their chances of living out the night in such a blow were becoming slim.

In the unequal fight, the hungry sea was bound to win, and a momentary relaxation of their vigilance would have seen them overturned by a snarling crest.

"What d'ye think of our chances for bein' picked up?" queried Jackson.

Thomas made no bones about his reply.

"Purty dam' small, Will. This blow 'll have sent all th' fishermen hereabouts aswingin' off for shelter. This flurry is only commencin', an' afore long it'll stiffen inter a rare ol' southeaster an' blow for days, maybe. I cal'late th' best we kin do is t' put th' dory before it an' make th' land. Seal Island lays 'bout fifty or sixty miles off —"

"A long run, Jimmy, in a sea like this."

"Aye, 'tis a long run, but better t' take th' chanst than blow aroun' out here."

"Any water in th' jar?"

"No, Will."

"Any grub in yer pockets?"

"Nawthin'."

Jackson bit off a quid and remarked phlegmatically, "Hell of a nice fix we're in, Jimmy. Shall I h'ist th' dory-sail an' let her run?"

"Aye, reef it an' set it. I'll steer."

For two long hours, under the small rag of sail, the little craft surged and swooped over the foam-laced seas in the Stygian darkness, and her two occupants communed with their thoughts. Both were married men with children and, as they drove through the night, a white sleet-covered phantom, their minds were full of the fancies which come to men facing death.

"This Winter fishin's no life for a man," remarked Jackson, after a lengthy interval.

"'Tis no life for any one that ain't a man," corrected Thomas. "It's takin' big chances an', Billy boy, it takes men with plenty of nerve t' do it. D'ye see anythin' ahead thar', Bill? My eyes are waterin' with starin' so long in th' dark, but I thought I saw a light t' loo'ard."

Jackson peered into the wall of blackness ahead and endeavored to pierce the opaque veil.

"Can't see a blame thing. It's black as the inside o' Tophet," he shouted.

Then the dory climbed over the shoulder of a cresting grayback and a red light flickered almost overhead.

"Round her up — an' quick!" yelled Jackson. "We're slammin' dead into a vessel, by th' Lord Harry —"

Crash! Into the port-broadside of a large schooner went the careering dory and, as she struck the hull, both men made a mighty leap for the vessel's rail and tumbled inboard upon a slush-covered deck.

"Wall, ef that ain't a hell of a way t' come aboard!" cried a man standing aft on the schooner's quarter. "Who's that anyway?"

"We're from th' *Winslow*," said Thomas when he had recovered his breath. "Made a night-set an' got adrift."

"Why, blast me, 'tis Jimmy Thomas," said a voice. "Say, you ol' scut, what kind of a night is this t' be makin' night-sets? Gittin' tired o' life? An' what d'ye mean by slappin' inter us like ye did? By th' Great Hook Block! I thought we were rammed by a blame' steamboat — "

"Keep a joggin', shipmate," answered the other. "What vessel's this anyway?"

"What vessel sh'd it be but th' *Camisoto* – th' newest an' best out of Anchorville. Come for'ard, you two, an' git interjuced. Oh, skipper! Here's a couple *Winslow* fellers blowed aboard. Didn't like their own craft so jest flew aboard here an', by th' same token, dam' near sinkin' us as they came alongside."

And after entering the foc'sle, they were greeted with rough courtesy by the *Camisoto's* skipper, Jim Costello, a huge redheaded Gloucester Irishman.

"Draw to, boys, an' mug-up. 'Tis a bitter night t' be adrift, an' I cal'late ye're lucky, ay, darn lucky, ye hit us th' way ye did, even ef ye came at us bows-on an' hell-fur-leather."

As the big skipper lurched past them on his way to the ladder, Thomas was distinctly aware of the odor of liquor and, when seated at the foc'sle table, it needed no great powers of observa-

tion to perceive that several of the gang lolling around were decid-
edly the worse for drink.

"Oho," muttered Jimmy to himself. "Fishin' must be high-line
when there's a kag o' rum floatin' around. Not but what it's a
good thing to have aboard a vessel winter fishin' – though I don't
like t' see *too* much of it on a vessel at sea. Especially with th'
gangs Jim Costello ships."

And Jimmy gave an ominous shake of the head.

III.

After a mug-up of hot beans, ginger-cake and coffee, the two dorymates were indulging in a soul-satisfying smoke when the skipper sent for them to come aft. Entering the cabin, they found the
place crowded with men smoking and playing cards on the lockers
and having, to all appearances, a good time. Thomas noted the
hour, one o'clock, and mentally disapproved of the two stone jugs
to which the uproarious gang were applying themselves.

"Come an' have a nip, boys!" bawled Costello, and his voice
boomed above the chatter of the carousers and the roar of wind
and sea. " 'Tis a little health we're drinkin' to th' vessel an' her
luck. What d'ye think o' her, fellers? She's a fine able craft, hey? I
cal'late neither th' *Winslow* nor Fred Hanson's sharp-hulled peddler
c'n show th' *Camisoto* a stern-wake. She kin trim anythin' aroun'
these coasts, sailin' or fishin', so she kin. Four days on th' grounds
an' a hunder' an' forty thousan' below. Kin' ye beat that, you *Winslow* men? Come on! Toss her off an' give th' ship a good name!"

Passing the stone jug over, Captain Costello commenced a
boastful dithyrambic upon the virtues of his new vessel, turning

every now and again for confirmation from one or other of the hard-looking crowd lolling upon the lockers.

They *were* a hard crowd, to say the least, for a tough skipper like Jim Costello always has a dare-devil, fearless gang of men trailing after him. They worked hard, lived hard and incidentally drank hard, and their reputations when ashore were unsavory. Bartenders on Atlantic Avenue, Boston, knew Costello's gang and telephoned for the police when they entered their saloons, while the rumsellers and "blind pig" proprietors in the baiting-ports of the North Shore and Treaty Coasts nerved themselves for trouble when they landed on their beaches.

As the two stone jars circulated, the crowd became argumentative and quarrelsome and, with no desire to become involved in a drunken discussion, Thomas and Jackson discreetly retired to the lockers aft of the companion-steps.

"George Morrissey must ha' bin a fool t' let Jim Costello take this fine vessel," remarked the old man. "Talked him inter it, I cal'late, with his tales o' high-line trips made by him an' his hard-driving gang o' Cape Bretoners an' six-foot Judique men. Eh, eh, Will, but I'm tired. 'Twas a hard day we had. Why, th' lad's asleep already."

Knocking the ashes out of his pipe, old Jimmy kicked his boots off, and threw himself down on the locker.

Though he essayed slumber many times, his mind persisted in remaining wakefully alert, and for over an hour he hung on the hardwood seat listening to the drunken roisterers aft and the whining roar of the wind overhead. The skipper had been silent for some little time, but at two in the morning he came out of his berth and lurched on deck. A few minutes later, he came below.

"Boys," he said, and old Jimmy listened in nervous apprehension to his words, "I cal'late we'd be doin' well ef we swung her off for home now. We've a full trip an' a high market t' run for, so when ye git a fair wind for home, take it, says I. Maybe we'll git a blasted no'wester t'-morrer that'll head us off in th' Bay an' keep us beatin' around for a week, so I cal'late we'll make a runnin'-trip outer this little southerly breeze an' swing off. Up on deck now, fellers, an' h'ist th' mains'l!"

Old Jimmy gave Jackson a prod with his foot.

"Will," he whispered, "d'ye hear what them crazy galoots are a-goin' t' do?"

"Naw!" growled Jackson sleepily.

"They're h'istin' th' mains'l to swing off! Can't ye hear them on deck thar'? Whole mains'l th' drunken swab is givin' her, in a blow like this, an' all hands as drunk as a fiddler's cat! He don't care a hoot for anythin'. Listen to him."

Down the open companion came Costello's hoarse voice:

"Jig her up, boys! Now give her th' jumbo. All ready! Swing her off, Danny! Start yer main-sheet, an' jibe yer fores'l!"

Crash! The foresail had been jibed without tackles, and the shock almost started the decks.

"That's th' style," continued Costello. "Her gear's new an' she'll stand it! No'th by west, Danny, an' drive her, you!"

Jackson was fully awake now. As the vessel swung off the wind, she rolled down and set the dorymates sliding to leeward.

"Holy Sailor!" cried Jackson. "I'm thinkin' we'd be better off in th' dory, after all. This feller 'll run her under or whip th' sticks over the side. Hark to th' wind."

"Ay, it's blowin' some, Will, An' we've got a kag o' rum pacin' th' quarter an' a kag o' rum to th' wheel. What was it that Gran' Manan lad used t' sing:

"A vessel goes under th' devil's thumb,
When th' skipper takes sights through a kag o' rum."

Costello clattered down into the cabin, the snowflakes melting on his beard and shoulders. "Hey, you *Winslow* fellers," he cried, with a hoarse laugh. "We'll give ye a chanst t' meet yer skipper a-comin' inter Anchorville wharf with his flags half-mast in yer honor!"

"Maybe," interrupted Thomas slowly, "but Cap'n Costello, I'd think more o' yer judgement ef ye'd ha' kept yer vessel lyin' to till daylight. On a night like this ye're runnin' a chanst o' half-mastin' more flags than the *Isabel Winslow's* —"

"Back to yer bunk, you ol' croaker!" cried Costello, sarcastically. "I kin run a vessel blind, drunk or sober. I cal'late ye think I'm drunk an' don't know what I'm a doin'?"

He straightened up to his full six feet and laughed.

"Ha! ha! I reckon ye're gittin' scared. This ain't the *Isabel Winslow*, with her kid skipper an' her longshore crowd o' farmers, an' don't forget it, my bully. You ain't asayin', 'Harry, me boy, I wouldn't do this' or 'Skipper, dear, 'tis a reef in our mains'l we sh'd be takin'!' You don't know me, old son. I'm th' rough, tough Jimmy Costello, see? An' me an' my ways are known from Eastern P'int to th' Treaty Shore, an' ef I kain't drive a vessel in any durn' breeze o' wind aroun' these coasts, I dunno who kin."

Almost unshipping the stovepipes as he lurched drunkenly against them, he reeled into his berth and tumbled, all standing, into his bunk.

"Call me ef it moderates," he cried, with a hoarse laugh at this old fisherman's joke.

IV.

With two Cape Breton Scotsmen to the wheel, the *Camisoto* was driving into the darkness with the speed of an express-train. It was terrifying, the manner in which the vessel stormed and swooped over the wind-hounded sea. With her great white main-sail full as a balloon with the pressure of the gale, the seventy-five foot boom bending like a bow and the main-sheet-ropes as taunt as bar-iron, the schooner tore through the cresting surges, and the foam caused by her onslaught roared by on either quarter in great, gleaming, effervescent streaks, which dimly illuminated the red, perspiring faces of the helmsmen.

Swash! With a hair-raising swoop, the over-driven vessel rammed her bowsprit into the back of a solid green comber and drove her bow under, clean to the foremast. Up she came again, steaming and spurting water from every scupper-hole and then, with half her keel out of water, squatted down on a racing, roaring grayback until she overtook another and drove bowsprit, anchors, windless and cable out of sight. The gang had retired to their bunks fore and aft, and the foc'sle crowd, with the scuttle drawn tight, were too drunk to pay any attention to the thundering seas which crashed overhead.

Thomas and Jackson squatted in the pen between house and kid and, to their sober eyes, the pace seemed fearful.

"Costello is carrying sail all right," Jimmy shouted in his dorymate's ears, "but I don't like this drivin' in for th' land on a night like this. I don't believe he took a sound afore he swung her off, an' he's put th' log over 'thout the fan on it. Look out!"

The vessel swung around to the push of a gigantic sea and the huge main-boom commenced topping up.

"She's a-goin' t' jibe!"

The two helmsmen managed by superhuman efforts to heave the wheel over as the sail gave a thunderous flap, but the task of keeping the wildly yawing vessel steady, in such a wind and sea, was beginning to have a sobering effect upon them. Three times they were within an ace of jibing, and a jibe then would have whipped the masts out of her and, when the strong kicking of the rudder wrenched their muscles and the wheel threatened to become unshipped from the patent gearing, the two Cape Bretoners had enough.

"Oh, there, skipper!" they bawled. "She's takin' charge of us! We can't hold her. Better git th' mains'l in —"

Costello came swearing to the deck.

"Take in nawthin'," he growled. "She's travelin' nicely. Below thar', come up an' relieve wheel! How far's she run? What's th' log read, Joe? Ain't no fans on it, ye say? Huh! T' blazes with it – they ain't no dam' good nohow!"

He jerked the instrument out of the becket and hove it over the side.

It was blowing hard by now, so hard that the new helmsmen were frightened, drunk and all as they were, and it did not take them long to sober up with the exertion of steering in the bitter snow-filled air. Will Jackson, unafraid in the dory a few hours before, was becoming nervous and Jimmy Thomas's words betrayed the fear in his heart.

"He's crazy, Will. Even ef they wanted to, they couldn't take that mains'l in, now. It's blowin' a whole gale now, an' her drivin' for th' land!"

"Let's go an' make him haul her up," cried the other.

"'Tis no use, lad. He's so chuck full of rum an' pride that he'd never listen to us an', ef I mistake not, a good deal o' this crackin'-on is fur our special benefit. He thinks we'll talk when we git t' home about his rough, bold ways, an' give him a devil of a name among the Anchorville folks. He's been asportin' aroun' with that Molly Letourneau, an' a yarn like this would make him th' very deuce o' a boy with th' brazen —"

Crash! The vessel shipped a solid sea which came careering aft, flooding the decks to the rail, and the helmsmen yelled in their fright.

"Hey thar, skipper, we kain't hold her!"

"No, blast ye, ye can't. Send McTavish, an' Jock Neale up, some one! Rouse 'em out! They'll sail her, by thunder, ef any one can!"

When two rough-looking creatures came on deck and grasped the spokes, the former helmsmen came forward to Thomas and Jackson.

"Skipper's gone crazy," they yelled. "Never knew him do this afore. Useter carry on some, but he's been drinkin' all th' time he's been on th' Bank."

The new helmsmen held her fairly steady, but the gait the vessel was making was proving too much for them. The wild swoops and yaws which she made instilled fear into their drink-obscured brains and, as they sobered up with the exertion of straining at the spokes, they began to realize the awful risk they were running.

Glancing down at the cabin-clock, Thomas saw it was five in the morning, and for three hours the schooner had been running on her north-by-west course. It was still dark, and blowing as hard as ever, and the snow shut out all sight within a hundred feet of the vessel. There was no watch forward; all hands except the skipper, the two at the wheel, the two just relieved and Thomas and Jackson, were below, and the schooner was driving in for the land at a sixteen-knot gait.

Costello, standing in the companion, leered tipsily at the little groups seated on the house and turned to his henchmen at the wheel.

"She kin sail, this vessel!" he roared. "Give it to her! Drive her! She's a new vessel an' her gear 'll stand it!"

And he started to shout a ribald chorus.

"Don't you reckon it's time t' haul up, skipper?" cried one of the relieved helmsmen. "She's been hittin' up an awful clip sence we swung off, an' I cal'late we were well to th' no'th'ard of the Bank when we put th' mains'l on her."

"Oh, is that so, Donald? An' when hev ye taken upon yerself t' keep track o' this vessel's courses? Who's sailin' her – you or me?"

"Naw!" yelled the man. "You're not sailin' her. 'Tis th' rotgut in yer skin that's crackin'-on, ye cursed drunken sweep!"

Whipping out a bait-knife from a cleat, he hove it with all his strength at the leering Costello.

The weapon caught the skipper on the shoulder and drove through the oilskin coat. With a roar like a maddened bull's Costello plucked the knife out, and leaping upon the house made for his assailant.

"I'll cut ye, my son," he screamed. "I'll make bait out o' yer hide, my bully!"

As he rushed for the man cowering behind the mainmast, old Jimmy threw himself upon the drink-crazed skipper and both rolled to the deck, snarling and cursing. Though Costello was a strong man, yet the old fisherman was as tough as an ox in spite of his fifty-odd years, and it did not take him five seconds to whisk the knife out of the skipper's hand.

"Stand up, now, you murderin' thief!" bawled Jimmy. "I'll trim you on her own deck an' take charge — "

For an almost unnoticeable space, he paused and then shouted harshly at the man rising to his feet.

"D' ye hear them, you scum? You've put a finish on things now, for, by God, ye're in among th' Ledges already!"

"Hard alee! Breakers ahead!" screamed a voice from forward, and the wind had scarce allowed the hail to reach the ears of the horrified listeners, when, surging madly forward on the back of a seething, roaring wall of black water, the vessel fetched up in her career with a fearful, staggering crash.

V.

Winslow swung his vessel off for home at midnight. The glass was ominously low and he had no heart for further fishing, after losing his two men. About five in the morning, after a wild night in which they furled the mainsail and drove for the land under a reefed foresail, he hauled to the wind and laid-to until daylight. The snow had ceased and it was just breaking dawn when the watch on deck called Winslow's attention to their dangerous proximity to the land.

"Ye kin see th' Cape from th' masthead, an' there's half a dozen o' them blame' ledges under our lee."

"How's th' Cape bearin'?"

"No'th by east, or thereabouts."

"Git th' ridin'-sail out an' bend it. Up on yer jumbo! We'll run for th' Bay by the inside passage. It'll be a clear run an' smoother water."

It was still blowing hard and a heavy, breaking sea was running, but daylight had robbed the storm of most of its terrors. Under the triangular riding-sail, the reefed foresail and jumbo, the *Isabel Winslow* swung off with her bowsprit pointing northwest by west and, running in the lee of a number of the dangerous underwater ledges which encircle the southern coast of Nova Scotia, she made good weather of the blow and drove for home at a twelve-knot gait.

The Salvage Rock gas and whistling buoy had just been left astern when the lookout hailed from the windlass.

"Vessel ashore on Durkee's Ledge!"

From foc'sle and cabin the gang came tumbling up, and Winslow, standing on the shearpole, scrutinized the vessel through his glasses.

"By th' Lord Harry! 'Tis the *Camisolo* – Jim Costello's craft – th' new one. Come up a little, Wally! Steady! Port a little! We'll run down to loo'ard an' see what we kin do. God help them! I'm afraid it's all over with her crowd!"

In a few minutes, the wrecked schooner was plainly visible from the *Isabel Winslow's* decks. She was lying over on her side – it was low water then – and the spray was bursting over her in steam-like clouds.

"Any one aboard her, skipper?" queried a dozen anxious voices.

"Ye-e-s! Seems t' me I see somethin' in th' main-riggin'. It may be a tangle o' broken gear. No! It's livin' men all right! They're wavin'! Let me think what I'd better do. I cal'late I'd better not risk heavin'-to around these ledges with th' blame' tides a-rippin' around them. I might git ashore myself. Cal'late we'll run up in th' lee o' th' Ledge an' anchor. Git a twenty-five fathom range over th' windlass an' see yer starb'd anchor clear for lettin' go. I'll take th' wheel, Wally. Sheet in, fellers!"

Lurching and pitching in the heavy rips running among the ledges, the schooner ran swiftly to leeward of the wreck and, coming to the wind, shot within a scant cable's length of the wave-swept menace.

"All ready, for'ard? Down jumbo an' fores'l! Let go your anchor!"

As the gang came aft, after seeing all snug, and the vessel riding easily in the lee of the ledge to her best anchor and one hundred and fifty feet of chain, Winslow addressed them:

"Thar's a half a dozen men in th' riggin', as far as I kin see through th' spray, an I cal'late th' best way t' git them is t' sling a couple dories over an' git them poor beggars t' slide down some o' th' lee gear from th' masthead. She's canted over on her bilge far enough for them t' do that ef they ain't froze stiff. Use your own judgment, boys, dories away!"

The words were hardly out of his mouth before a rush was made for the dory-tackles, and before Winslow could remonstrate, the gripes were off, and four dories were over the rail, while others were being hastily made ready.

"That'll do, fellers! No need for all hands t' go! Lord save us! Ye'd think 'twas a liner ashore, with th' Government boat a thousand miles away!"

Crowding the rail, the gang watched the work of the rescuers with anxious eyes. A running fire of comments and ejaculations told of the excitement possessing them:

"Good boy, Henderson! He's got one feller! They're comin' down th' lee riggin' an' jumpin for th' dory. He's fallen short – Burke's grabbed him – gaffed him like a halibut, by Christopher! How many is there? Six? Seven, ye say? God ha' mercy on th' rest! Wonder ef th' skipper is among them. Lucky thing th' masts stood when she struck!"

"Stand by, now, fellers!" cried Winslow.

The four boats came surging down, impelled by the strong arms of the rowers, and it was evident that only seven of the *Camisoto's* gang had been saved. Henderson's dory was in advance of the rest and he hailed Winslow from a distance.

"Hey, skipper!" he yelled. "Look who's here!"

As Winslow stared at the two heads appearing over the dory-gunwale, he made out the familiar features of his two lost men – Jimmy Thomas and Will Jackson!

With an exultant, boyish whoop, the young skipper grabbed old Jimmy as he came over the rail and, as the men afterward said, "A'most climbed all over ol' Jimmy's frame, an' cussed sinful!"

"Oh, you darned ol' tough! What d'ye mean by runnin' away from me on Brown's an' a'most scarin' me t' death? Dam' my eyes! I don't know whether I sh'd turn to an' lick th' two o' ye or — But I might ha' known that no skipper c'd lose sich a pair o' ugly, ornery cusses – ye'd sure git picked up. Oh, Jimmy, but I spent a black night – aye, a bitter night! How'd it all happen – this wreck, I mean?"

The old man passed his hands over his eyes wearily. He too had spent a black night and it pressed upon him.

"Oh, Harry-boy, take an old man's advice an' never go ship-mates with a kag o' rum. Aye! I don't like t' pass word upon dead men, but if Jim Costello had left his stone jars ashore he'd ha' been alive now – him an' eighteen men.

"How'd he come away in here? He was with us on Brown's last night."

"Drunk, Harry. Wanted t' show off. H'isted th' whole mains'l on her at two this mornin' an' drove her, aye, hove th' log away, took no soundin's, but drove her slam-bang before it until an hour ago, when she fetched up on th' Ledge. When she struck, th' port-dories and th' cable came over on the foc'sle hatch an jammed th' gang below. Eighteen men died in that foc'sle – drowned like rats in a trap – for her bows were under until th' tide fell. Jim Costello was the last to go. Says t' me when he saw what happened:

" 'Waal, I cal'late I've done it now. Ef ye git clear, give my love t' Molly Letourneau an' tell George Morrissey that th' *Camiso-to* was th' best vessel at runnin' that I ever knowed.'"

"That was all he said, an' with that he jumps over th' rail. He was a hard case, Harry – an awful hard case, an' may God have mercy on his soul, for he has many sins to answer for."

"Amen to that!" ejaculated Winslow solemnly.

"I cal'late I'll go below. Sorry I lost th' dory, skipper —"

"Dam' th' dory! I'd sooner lose a thousand dories than lose you an' Jackson. Go below an' turn in. We'll look after them other poor fellers, an' 'tis in Anchorville we'll be tonight, thank th' Lord!"

VI.

They were not destined to make Anchorville that night. Things happen quickly at sea, and while the *Isabel Winslow* had been engaged in the work of rescue, the southeaster had suddenly shifted to the northwest. Instead of riding easily in the lee of Durkee's Ledge, the schooner was now swinging with the Ledge on her port-beam and her bowsprit pointing due west. Astern, some three miles away, lay the long line of breakers betokening the shoal-water of the dangerous Crescent Reef, while to starboard, the St. Paul's, Old Man, John Island and Eudora Ledges practically prohibited navigation among them in anything but a smooth sea and a favoring wind and tide.

Winslow noticed this; noted the direction of the wind; the barometer rising from the low pressure of twenty-nine and the falling thermometer.

"Huh! More dirt," he muttered. "We'll git it good an' strong soon, an' us jammed down among them ledges. Ef I kin hang on here till th' wind comes more to th' no'th or till ebb-tide, I kin git out easily, but now we're jammed in a clinch. On deck thar! Give her more chain – ten fathom."

While the skipper studied the compass with visible concern, the wind came away in vicious squalls which caused the schooner to wrench at her chain and fetch up on the windlass with grinding jerks. It was rapidly becoming colder; the slushy sleet of the southeaster changed with the wind into stinging hard-grained snow and the spray which swashed up over the bows froze on bowsprit gear and windlass.

"Goin' t' be violent, skipper," remarked Jimmy Thomas, coming on deck. "Glass risin' quick after being low means dirty, sharp weather ahead – wind from th' no'th'ard most likely. Nasty place we're in!"

"I know it. I cal'late we'll give her more chain. She's fetchin' up hard now, an' I'm afraid she'll yank th' windlass outer her. Th' tide's settin' agin us mighty strong. All up, fellers! Bend on th' hawser to th' port anchor an' cockbill it all ready t' let go! Give her th' full scope of th' chain when ye've done that!"

It was blowing hard now and no error. Squall after squall came whirling down, accompanied by skin-cutting hail and snow, and the schooner staggered to their onslaught. All around them, the ledges and reefs were creaming in acres of white water, and the decks of the fishing schooner were rapidly filming with ice. The men, over-hauling the cable, slipped and slithered around on the glazed planks and cursed the bitter cold, as with numb fingers they beat and hammered the frozen links out of the chain-box and wrestled with an eight-inch manila fishing-hawser almost solidly welded to the cable-rack.

Clank-clink-clank! went the heavy links as the men threw them over the barrel. *Crash!* And the anchor took up the slack. Out to the end they paid it, then some one hove over one turn too much. *Cr—r-runch!* The vessel made a savage lurch and, before the men could stop it, the turns spun around the iron-shod barrel and in a sputter of sparks the chain slipped through the hawse-pipe.

"Chain's gone!" yelled some one.

"Over with th' port-anchor for the love o' God!" roared Winslow, and Henderson cut the ring-stopper with the ax.

Shying down to leeward, the great yellow cable crawled over the side, and the schooner swung around with a terrific jerk, as the hawser tautened and the anchor bit the bottom.

"Give her all th' line ye've got!" cried Winslow, "an' see that yer end is made fast."

The hawser, six hundred feet of it, was all that was holding them now, and if that parted – well –

As he thought of the possibility, Winslow glanced over at the now dismasted hulk of the *Camisoto*, rapidly pounding to pieces.

"Lord grant that it holds," he murmured, "or there'll be many widows in Anchorville within the hour."

Another squall whirled down and the reefs around them vanished in the gray-white of a snow storm. From the bows came the ominous hail:

"She's draggin', skipper!"

Winslow ran forward.

"Draggin' ye say? Are ye sure, John? Give me a dory-compass. Durkee's Ledge was 'bout sou'-b'-west. How's she bearin' now? Sou'west ye say? Holy Sailor! She's trailin' that anchor like a piece o' string."

The wind was blowing heavier every minute and the flood-tide was swirling hard against them.

"We're goin' on th' reef, skipper," said old Jimmy. "Onless th' wind shifts or eases up, we're done for!"

The men had gathered aft now and were looking to the young skipper for orders. For an instant he gazed around the stolid, wind-bronzed faces, and his brain worked quickly.

"Where's that Cobtown Harbor man?" he barked.

"Here, sir!"

"You know this locality?"

"Fished around here some in motor-boats."

Winslow jumped below and brought up a chart. Laying it out upon the top of the house, he held a rapid consultation with the fisherman from Cobtown Harbor, and made up his mind.

"Waal, fellers," he said calmly, "ye kin see how we're fixed. I can't beat out o' here, 'cause o' wind an' tide, an' ef we hang to anchor we'll go ashore on th' Crescent Reef astern thar. I'm agoin' t' take a chance – a fightin' chance, an Lord help us! Up on th' ridin'-sail! Is that kedge all ready? All right, now – give her fores'l an' jumbo!"

The men jumped to obey orders with a blind faith in the young skipper's ability to pull them through, although they hadn't the faintest idea of what he intended to do.

As soon as the riding-sail was hoisted, Winslow called the Cobtown man to the lee-wheel and both lashed themselves to the box.

"Cut yer cable for'ard!" roared the skipper and, as Thomas severed the great rope with two cuts of the ax, the jumbo bellied to the breeze and the schooner fell off, with her bowsprit pointing to the fuming reefs to starboard.

Was he going to try and weather the reefs? The gang wondered for an instant, but the next order dispelled the supposition.

"Slack away yer fore-sheet!"

The skipper and the Cobtown man rolled the wheel over.

"Now, thar', fellers, git below, or lash yourselves to th' riggin'. Draw all slides tight. The *Isabel Winslow* 'll show her qualities this day afore we're through. Over with th' wheel!"

"My God, skipper!" yelled a man in amazement, "ye're putting her dead afore it an' slammin' for th' reef!"

"Aye! I'm doin' now on purpose what Jim Costello did in recklessness, but while he lost men, I'm tryin' t' save them. Steady th' helm!"

Like a hound released from leash, the schooner caught the fury of a squall in her sails and bounded for the whirling chaos of maddened water which marked the long crescent-shaped ledge. Standing on the house and at the heel of the mainmast, the men, lashed to boom and fife-rail, stared in fascinated horror at the rapidly nearing breakers, and, speechless, mentally ticked off the seconds they had to live.

The vessel seemed to have become imbued with life. She rose steadily on the crest of a sea. With a trembling in every timber, she rushed down the seething declivity with a roar, defiant, like a charger stamping into the fray. Flinging the water off her flooded decks, she stormed forward, irresistible in her onslaught. The two at the wheel braced themselves against their lashings; Winslow, with puckered brows, staring calmly ahead, and his helper iron-jawed and desperate.

Crash! A huge sea toppled over the stern and the helmsmen vanished under a foam-streaked cataract of bitter, wind-whipped water. Quickly it sluiced away, and the oil-skinned figures emerged, undismayed and still at their post.

The blue-black of the sea was changing to the emerald green of broken water. The roar of the surf was in the ears of the men hanging to the rail and boom. They were now in among the breakers, which toppled over the rail on either side, while a great, translucent wall of brilliant emerald rose astern and threatened to overwhelm them. It wavered for an instant, broke and careered by on either quarter. Up, up, up, went the schooner, her bowsprit pointing to the lowering sky, then sky, sea and vessel were blotted out as the men went under in a deluge of icy water.

Cr-r-unch! The schooner struck, staggered for an instant, and drove on.

Crash! Another fearful shock and a deluge of raging sea. Men gasped for breath, and, with bursting lungs, murmured choked farewells to the ones at home, while the maddened elements snatched at their numb, frozen bodies and tried to tear them away from their lashings.

For a brief instant they drew breath, listened to the thunder of the surf and gazed upon the fearsome hell of waters which raged around them. Another deluge, and each man felt he was being torn asunder. In their ears rang the sounds heard only by those pressed under by a sea; when lungs expand to breaking, when the breath escapes hissing through the clenched teeth, eyes see red and the mind calls to the tortured muscles to "Let go! Let go!"

At last she came up. It was strangely quiet.

"Was this death?" men asked, till the skipper's voice broke harshly upon the ear.

"All right, fellers! Down fores'l an' jumbo! Leggo yer kedge!"

They had driven clear across the reef!

"Aye! It was our only chance," Winslow was saying. "She couldn't weather any o' them ledges and even cuttin' away th' sticks wouldn't ha' kept her from draggin'. I knew thar must be some place aroun' here whar' a vessel might scrape over an' when Tom Jenkins here tells me 'bout thar bein' two fathoms on th' southwest horn o' th' reef at high water, I jest slams her over it, trustin' that she'd strike easy. I cal'late she's ground her skag t' flinders. I c'n see pieces of it a-comin' up now —"

With the reaction coming after such a strain, he started to laugh hysterically. "Ha! ha! She's done some poundin' this day.

Poor Jim Costello – nineteen men gone t' hell for a jug o' rum!
Oh! It's a cruel life – a dog's life!"

And he dropped in a heap upon the ice-covered deck.

They hung to the little kedge in the lee of the reef until the gale
moderated, and next morning came into Anchorville Bay iced up
to the foremasthead and with all the gang spelling at the pumps.
She was leaking, but not as much as would be expected from a
vessel which had banged her way over a shoal-water reef in a winter's gale.

It had been a wild week at sea and the flags on the Court-
House and Post-Office were at half-mast for many of Anchorville's sons. The *Camisoto* was gone, with her skipper and eighteen
men. The *Clara Willis* was strewing the rocks of Grand Manan
with her wreckage, and two dories had failed to answer the muster
when her survivors made the beach. Fred Hanson, in the *Minnehaha*, had lost two men reefing the mainsail on Brown's, while Bill
McCall, in the *Senator Vincent*, had lost his mainmast off the Seal
Island, and had to be towed into Yarmouth after a night when all
had given themselves up for lost.

It was a week of gnawing anxiety to those who had hus-
bands, sons, fathers, and brothers at sea, and, when the *Winslow*
came in, battered and storm-worn, they breathed heartfelt thanks
unto the Almighty for the safety of another vessel.

"And what did you make out of it, Harry?" the skipper's pretty
wife asked him two days later. All Anchorville knew the story of

the *Winslow's* trip and Isabel Winslow had heard the tale from other than the reluctant lips of her husband.

"Waal, sweetheart," answered the young skipper with a laugh, "fish prices are runnin' high these days an' I cal'late th' gang ain't growlin' over th' seventy dollars they drawed. I might ha' made a hundred, an' I cal'late 'twould be a good idea t' take a little holiday, you and I, while th' vessel is on th' railway!"

"A hundred dollars!" cried his wife with a note in her voice that Winslow had never heard before. "And what is a paltry hundred dollars to the wives and children of men who live such a life? What is a hundred dollars in the scale against the dead of the *Camisoto* – nineteen men – and the poor Anchorville boys lost on the *Minnehaha* and the *Willis?* And the chance you took! Driving over that reef! What if you had struck? Did you ever think of that? Look at the risks you have been running those ten days at sea – and all for a hundred dollars! Oh, Harry, but it's cruel work, and I'm all the time afraid some one will come to my door and tell me my husband's gone —"

"Ha! ha!" laughed the young skipper, clasping his sobbing wife in his strong arms. "Don't think on it, dearie! Even though we did hev a more than ornery exciting trip, yet a hundred dollars for ten days' work ain't t' be sneezed at. No siree!"

Like a Proper Sailorman!

I first noticed him eyeing the ship at a distance — a furtive scrutiny, as if he were afraid someone would catch him in the act. At first, I took him for an old watchman keeping guard over the deals on the dock, but latterly my curiosity was aroused by the manner in which he bobbed back among the deal stacks whenever our Skipper or any of the mates appeared on the deck or the wharf.

He was a very old man and he had all the earmarks of a sailor. I sized him up for that when he spoke to me at the head of the wharf one night. His gnarled right hand, holding the lapels of his ragged coat across his chest, had an eight-pointed star tattooed upon the back of it. Only sailors dare flaunt these barbaric decorations. Your landsman always keeps such weaknesses hidden.

A shore chum and I were yarning when the old fellow slouched into the glare of the arc-light. His feet, clad in sorry boots, scuffed with the drag of age; his shoulders had a hunched stoop proclaiming the curvature of years, while the lagging manner of his walk told of stiffened joints and muscles responding but slowly to the impulse of the brain.

He straightened up as he entered the circle of light and hearing our voices, he peered into the shadows where we sat. He stood for a moment irresolute as if he were debating in his mind how to act. Then with something of a jaunty roll in his gait he came towards us. "'Night, mates," he ventured – somewhat apprehensively, I thought – and his smile revealed two stumps of teeth in the upper jaw which gave his speech a sibilant lisp. "Cold night, eh?"

"Aye, it's a bit chilly, friend," returned my companion.

The old man clutched his coat lapels tighter and shivered. His face was the colour of antique ivory – a yellowy white as though the blood-flush had receded from a tanned skin. I noticed that he had gold wire rings in his ears – a fancy of old-time seafarers.

"When's th' wind-bag sailin'?" he enquired after a pause.

"Finish stowing in the 'tween decks tomorrow," I replied. "Ought to pull out in two or three days."

"Any deck-load?"

"Not this time of the year – November – winter, North Atlantic. Not allowed going to England," I answered tersely.

"Sure, sure! I forgot," he said hastily and then half-fearfully. "You on her, sir?" (I laughed at the "sir." He took me for an officer.)

"Aye, I'm on her, but I'm for'ad. An A.B. shipped for the run from Halifax to Sharpness."

"Oh!" There was a sigh of relief in that "Oh!" He stood quiet for a moment as if thinking over his next move. Then he burst out. "Say, matey, put an old-timer wise. I want to git out of this here Halifax. I've tried to ship this two months past but none o' them mates or skippers'll take me. Say I'm too old. I ain't too old, mate. Only fifty-four, s'help me, and I can do me work – hand, reef, steer, 'n' heave th' lead. I bin bos'un in big ships – wind-jammers. I know my book. Never shipped in steam – always th' wind-bags. Must git away now. I'm broke. Skinned to the ballast. Now, son, tell me! Have you got yer crowd yet?"

There was a note of pathetic appeal in his lisping voice – a hoarse supplication. Fifty-four? The aged liar was seventy-four if he was a day, but these worn-out shell-backs always lie about their age. I wouldn't blame any mate or master for not signing him on. He was too old for work in a sailing ship – especially a timber drogher making a winter passage of the Western Ocean.

"We've ten hands to get yet," I replied.

He gave a series of pleased nods at the information. "Now, tell me, son," he said, lowering his voice into a lisping whisper. "Who takes the hands on? Th' skipper or th' mate?"

"The mate."

He grunted. "Is that th' feller with th' red moustache? Wears a grey sweater coat and a green felt hat?"

"That's him," I answered, and I thought to myself, "You've been watching the ship pretty closely to have got the mate's description down so pat."

"Now, tell me, son," he enquired in the same eager whisper, "d'ye think he'll gimme a chance? I aint' too old, y'know. Only fifty-four. Bin sick – roomatic fever – all right now . . . spry as ever. What's my chances?"

"You're pretty weak-looking," I ventured. I was going to say "old-looking," but changed my words.

He straightened his shoulders back and slapped his chest. When he released his coat lapels I saw that he had no shirt on – nothing but a cotton singlet and it was November and chill. "Weak-lookin'?" he almost shouted. "Why, damn yer eyes, young feller, I'll tie up a lee yard-arm and be layin' down afore you've got a gasket passed on th' weather one; and you know all th' weight's to loo'ard. Weak-lookin' be damned!" he said, instantly mollified. "I reckon I *look* weak, but I bin sick. Malaria, y'know. Got a touch one-time . . . Congo River. Now, tell me, m'lad! When's th' best time to see Mister Mate? Just after breakfast, ye say? Good! I'll see him in th' mornin'." He clutched his ragged coat again. "Say, pal, you'll do an old-timer a favour and you won't tip th' mate off about me." He spoke half-fearfully. "You won't tell him that an old crock is goin' to ask him for a chance in th' mornin'? I'm only fif-ty-four, s'help me, I am, an' fifty-four ain't old for a sailor. And, pal," his voice held a half-shamed appeal, "lend me a dollar to git a shirt 'n a bite 'n a haircut. I'll pay ye back – honest, I will – but I got to have a hair-cut." He half-raised his shabby soft hat and re-vealed a head thinly covered with snow-white hair. "I'll have to take off me hat, maybe, when I see yer mate, and if he sees me hair he won't believe I'm only fifty-four and he might turn me down. A dollar'll fix me up fine."

There was something so irresistibly pathetic in the man's plea – a wistful cajoling that brooked no refusal – that I parted with a dollar. He accepted it with a murmur of thanks – not the servile mumblings of the professional pan-handler – but rather the terse acknowledgement of one who hated to beg. I felt no reluctance in giving the old fellow the money, even though it left me with but fifty cents to tide me over till sailing day.

He jammed his hat well down over his head and clutching his coat tighter over his ill-clad chest, he shuffled around and faced the chill wind. "Well, so long, boys. I'll shove off now and I'll see Mister Mate in th' mornin'." And he slouched into the darkness with a sad attempt at a jaunty bearing to which his ancient frame refused response.

My companion laughed. "You're easy," he observed. "You'll never see him or your dollar again." But he was a landsman and with all of a landsman's suspicion. He noticed that the man did not address him in his plea for money and remarked upon the fact. "He knew he could get it easy out of a sailor. He didn't try to work *me*." He concluded with a sophisticated "Huh!"

"No," I returned slowly; "he wouldn't ask *you* for money. He's a *sailor*. I'll see him again." My shore friend, never having slept or eaten in a ship's fo'c'sle, did not comprehend the niceties of sea-farer's charity. A sailor will beg and borrow from sailors, but would scorn to do so from landsmen. There is an excess of delicacy in such matters that only seamen can understand.

I looked for him around the deal stacks early next morning, for I had a notion to invite him into the fo'c'sle and give him a bite to eat. But he wasn't in sight anywhere, though I surmised that he slept somewhere in the timber. Breakfast was served in the cabin at eight and the mate invariably smoked a cigarette, lounging in the main-deck entrance to the cabin, immediately after the meal.

The mate carried out his habit according to schedule and I glanced up the wharf for a sign of my old friend of the previous night. From amongst the longshoremen on the dock, he finally appeared and I saw him sight the mate under the poop-break. He came along the wharf with a jaunty swing and as he neared me I noticed that he had a muffler around his neck and that his hair was cropped close. The lagging step was gone and his shoulders were straightened a little, but he could not disguise the stoop. However, a good many sailors carrry a stoop – the trade-mark of years of bending and hauling – and it would probably pass notice.

He ignored the gangway amidships and walked abreast of the poop-break. The mate was regarding him idly and the old fellow noticed it. He imperceptibly charged his gait with more spring and leaped easily from the dock-string-piece to the ship's topgallant-rail. Along the rail he walked for a few steps and then swung down to the poop ladder and to the deck. I was working at the after-hatch and watched events with genuine curiosity – the more because of the pity of the ancient sailor's carefully planned strategy.

As he approached the officer, I noted a flush in his cheeks and a brightness in his faded blue eyes which told of stimulant. The man had evidently rejuvenated himself with a few stiff drinks ere coming down. The jaunty carriage bespoke artificial impulse.

"'Morn, Mister Mate," he said with a confident timbre in his voice. "Need a hand, sir?"

The officer looked keenly at him and the old fellow stood as erect as a soldier on parade under the scrutiny.

"You're pretty old," observed the mate quietly.

"Fifty-four, sir," replied the other quickly, " 'n' jest as spry, sir, as any you got for'ad. Got fever, years ago. . . . Gulf of Siam trade . . . aged me up, sir. You'll find me able enough, sir, when there's seaman's work to be done."

The other grunted.

"Let me see your last discharges!"

The man fumbled in an inside pocket and produced a bundle of soiled papers. From amongst them he produced the familiar blue-covered Discharge Book of the British Board of Trade. The mate took this and turned the pages slowly. From the vicinity of the after-hatch I watched the proceedings with almost as much trepidation as the old man, and I inwardly prayed that his last skipper had paid him off with a "V.G." for ability and conduct.

"You came out in the *Glen Corrie* – a one-time Scotch ship – three months ago — " remarked the officer. The other tried to avoid the coming question and parried hastily. "Yes, sir. A fine ship . . . one of Steele's old Australia-men. Th' Norwegians have her now, sir. Fine ship to handle . . . steers like a witch. I — "

"Why didn't you stand by her?" the other questioned, ignoring the interruption.

"Took a fancy to work ashore, sir. Been riggin' schooners, sir. I'm a dab at riggin', sir. Splice any kind o' wire, sir — " He was extolling his abilities and avoiding the truth. He was probably landed from his last ship into hospital – coopered up and worn out. Norwegians had no use for ancient seamen unable to stand the grind.

The officer handed the book back and lit another cigarette. "You're pretty weak-looking," he remarked. I gave a mental start at the designation. I had used the same term to cover a harsher word and I felt instinctively that the mate was doing the same. There is a kindly delicacy among sailors.

The aged sailorman slapped his chest with the same indignant motion of the night before. "Me, sir?" he barked. "Me, weak?" He glanced around as if to find something to prove his strength. Then he made a bold bid. "I ain't as spry as a boy, maybe, Mister, but I'll shin up the main there an' reeve a halyard through th' truck right now, sir!"

The mate smiled and looked him over and the other stood as if ready to run for the main-rigging and nip aloft.

Our mate wasn't an impressionable fellow by any means. He demanded a lot from his crowd and believed in hard work – with the accent on the "hard." Lazy men and shirkers received scant mercy at his hands. But the mate must have had a kindly impulse that morning. He finally threw his cigarette away and said, "All right. I'll take you as an A.B. Be at the Shipping Office at two o'clock. I think I'm a damn fool to carry an old crock like you, but I'll give you a chance."

The aged shellback's pride seemed nettled and he straightened up again. "I ain't no 'old crock,' mister. I can do my work. I bin bo'sun in big ships – wind-jammers – four-masters an' twenty-eight hundred tons. I bin — "

The officer made a gesture of dismissal. "All right. I believe you. Shove off now and be at the Shipping Office at two." And he entered the cabin. The old sailor caught my eye and favoured me with a knowing wink. It said a lot, that wink. He glanced sea-man-like around the decks and aloft at the rigging and spars. Then with a satisfied nod to himself, he made for the gangway and on to the wharf.

The last deal had been stowed below decks and we had hauled out into the stream to prepare for sailing when my elderly friend came aboard. A motor-boat ran him out and he scrambled up the Jacob's ladder along with two or three other hands. When he came into the fo'c'sle he was lugging an attenuated canvas sea-bag and by the look of him he was more than half drunk. Spying me, he lurched over and held out a crumpled dollar bill. "Here y' are, son," he lisped slurringly. "Thank ye kindly. 'M all ri' now."

But he didn't look all right. The eyes of him burned feverish-ly and there was a hectic flush on his ivory-yellow cheeks and once or twice I noticed him spitting blood. The new hands were quarrelling about the choice of bunks when he interrupted. "Stow yer jaw, you men," he commanded truculently. "You fellers'll take what I leaves. I'm takin' this pew here." And he threw his cap and bag into the best located of the bunks under dispute.

"Th' noive of de old guy!" ejaculated an ordinary seaman. The old man whirled on him. "Belay yer bazoo, you!" he barked threateningly, "or I'll put a stopper on it myself. It's a dam' fine time o'day when young cubs like you have so much to say. I've had more salt water on my oilskins than you ever sailed on, so, shove off, or I'll mark ye!" The fierceness of the old man's visage cowed the other and he made no reply. But Williams (that was his name) was wound up to talk and he held forth to the crowd at large. "In my day," he grumbled, "no ruddy ord'nary seaman was allowed to open his trap when A.B.'s were around. 'N when I was in the *Ariel* in the ol' days, the ord'naries was jest fetch'n-carry lads to us A.B.'s. Mind the *Ariel*, you fellers? I reckon not! You wasn't thought of then. China clipper she was 'n I was in her. Mind th' big race? *Taeping, Serica, Fiery Cross, Taitsing*, 'n *Ariel* . . . ninety-nine days from the Pagoda anchorage at Foochow to the Downs. That was sailin' m'lads."

I pricked up my ears at his talk, and being something of a student of nautical history, I recognized the names of the ships and the race he was referring to – the famous tea-clipper race of 1866, when the five ships mentioned left Foochow almost together and arrived off the Downs in the English Channel within a few hours of one another! And Williams boasted of being an A.B. in the *Ariel* – winner of the famous contest! And that was forty-eight years ago and he swore his age was fifty-four! I felt that my estimate of seventy-four was about right. The poor old devil!

The liquor in him had loosened his tongue and he was lisping valiantly. "You fellows don't know what sailorin' is nowadays," he continued scornfully. "Stuns'ls, Jimmy Greens, save-alls, water-sails, an' ring-tails . . . ye never heard o' them, I'll bet. 'N I was in th' best of them! Western Ocean packets, West Indiamen, China clippers, Cape Horners, an' Australian wool-clippers . . . I sailed in 'em all in my day. I was in th' old *Thermopylae*, I was, when she run from Melb'un in sixty-three days. I bin in th' *Cutty Sark*, I bin bo'sun in Blue Nose ships – tough packets where a man had to be a sailor or th' mates made shark's meat out o' you! Yes, I bin through th' damned mill, I have, 'n there's no swankin' ord'nary seaman what's goin' to give me any chin!" And he glared fiercely at the young fellow again.

He opened his sea-bag and turned it up. A dilapidated suit of yellow oilskins – picked up on a fish-wharf by the look and smell of them – and a thin grimy blanket fell out. He had nothing else. He hung the oil skins up alongside his bunk and hove the blanket into his sleeping box.

"You haven't much of a kit," I remarked to him quietly.

He nodded slowly. "Aye! A parish rig, son, but it'll do me, I reckon. I won't need 'em long." He lisped the words so low that none of the others heard, but the significance of it impressed me.

Next morning we got our anchor and towed out to sea and the tug let go the hawser off the Sambro light-ship. When making sail, old Williams was invariably the foremost hand at a halyard or brace and the ablest men gave way to him. When he came panting up to a pulling or hauling job we always gave him a "fore-all" place even though he was so weak that one could hardly feel his weight on the rope. Occasionally he would sing out the hauling time in a hoarse, cracked voice – an "E-yah! O hah! Hey-yah!" – but he generally had to knock off for want of breath. He essayed a chantey on the t'gallant halyards one day, but it was so ancient that no one could sing the chorus. The poor old man was living in the past.

As the time passed he seemed to age visibly. One could almost see him shriveling up. His motions were daily becoming more feeble and the only thing about him which showed a spark of vitality was the fire in his eyes. His speech even became more shrill and there was a querulous quaver in it. Matching the fierce glare in his eyes, his temper became fiery. He cursed everyone and criticized everything in a kind of petulant contempt.

We were hauling aft the main-sheet one day in mid-Atlantic when he collapsed and fell to the deck. He tried to rise to his feet and tally on, but couldn't muster the effort. "Carry him into his bunk," ordered the mate kindly, "and let him stay there!"

"Bunk be damned, mister!" shrieked the old fellow. "I'll be all right with a little shot o'rum, mister. I jest took a faint spell." But the officer noticed the red trickle at the corner of Williams' mouth and motioned us to carry him forward. We laid him in his bunk to the accompaniment of his shrill curses and there was no more heft to him than to a child.

The skipper ordered the steward to give him milk and rum and soft food. He drank the liquor but refused to touch the boiled rice and tapioca. "Think I'm a damned baby," he piped viciously. "You've a damned cheek to offer me that muck, you damned stew-pot walloper!" He condemned the steward to all eternity.

All that night he raved and shouted of long-forgotten ships and the men who sailed them. The famous clippers of fo'c'sle story were mentioned in his talk – *Leander, Sir Lancelot, Cairngorm, Stornoway* – brave ships of brave days. One moment he fancied he was setting a topgallant studdingsail and shouted commands long forgotten in sail of to-day; another time he was cautioning a phantom mate at a lee-wheel when running the Easting down in the Southern Ocean. "Meet her, bully! Don't let her swing! Never mind squintin' at th' big sea astern. Watch th' ship!"

He lay thus for many days until we met up with a dirty easterly roaring out of the British Channel. All night long we stripped her in the rain and bitter wind until we had her snugged down and lying-to under fore and main lower-tops'l and foretopmast stays'l.

With the coming of the gale, old Williams seemed to revive and when I looked in at him at four bells in the morning watch, he asked for a mug of coffee. I brought him the drink and asked how he was. "Better, son, better," he croaked. "But I ain't agoin' to set foot on shore again. I'm goin' out this time . . . on deep water. No more shore for me. I'm through with it. Done with it. I was always all right at sea. Th' shore has burned th' guts 'n th' heart out o' me. I made my money at sea and I spent it ashore. Th' rum, son, th' rum. Sixty years at sea, m'lad, an' here I am with niver a home or a wife or a dollar. A suit o' rags, a blanket, 'n a bunch o' discharges – that's all to show for it. But I've had my fun, son. I don't regret it. I sailed in th' best and th' worst. I know seafarin'. Sixty years an' never in steam. Always in th' wind-bags. Never in steam, so, d'ye hear? Never in steam. No steam-boats for Jim Williams."

I left him then and went on deck. He gave me something to think about. Sixty years at sea! A long time, truly. Old Williams had seen the life as it was in the roaring days of the clipper sailers. Sixty years . . . and he had nothing but his memories. He would be the last of them – the stun's'l shellbacks – the men of iron who drove the wooden ships. Nowadays the ships were iron and the men were wood.

It blew hard and dirty all day and the dark came down with the ship tumbling in a heavy sea and the wind screaming in the gear aloft as she rolled to windward. We were standing-by in the donkey-boiler house sheltering from the rain and wind when there came a thunderous slatting from aloft. The noise brought us out on deck as a great length of chain-sheet came rattling down, and up in the blackness one could hear the flogging of canvas and the slashing of a chain on an iron yard. Sparks of fire followed each metallic slash and someone shouted, "Weather sheet of th' main-tops'l has carried away!" The mate's whistle shrilled in the noise and the man who had answered it came for'ard. "Man th' weather gear!" he bawled. "Clew her up and make fast!"

The crowd of us tallied on to the bunt-lines and clew-lines and hove the weather-side of the sail up to the yard and then clawed our way up the weather rigging with the wind disputing our climbing and the rain slashing at our oilskins. We gained the lower-tops'l-yard, the whole watch of us, and strung out on the foot-ropes to fist the wet canvas, full of wind, and bellying back over the spar. It was as black as the inside of a sea-boot aloft and you couldn't tell who was next to you.

I was tugging away at the weather-yard-arm when I was conscious of a body squeezing in alongside of me. I had just taken a turn with the gasket and shouted to my neighbour to reach down under the yard and pass the end of the gasket up to me again. A querulous voice answered. "All right! All right, I'll get it!" Peering for the first time at the figure now crouching down on the foot-rope reaching for the gasket, I was astonished to make out the form of old Jim Williams!

When he stood up again I shouted in his ear, "Get down! Get down! You'll be falling to the deck!"

He was lying over the yard with both hands grasping the iron jack-stay. His head was bare – I could see his white hair in the gloom – and he had neither boots nor oilskins on. His coat and pants were bellying and flapping in the wind. He lay motionless.

I made my gasket fast in double quick time that I might attend to the old fellow. I was afraid that he had gone out in the effort of climbing aloft and lying out on the yard, but when I shook him gently by the shoulder, he lifted a hand from the jack-stay as if in protest and his thin voice piped faintly, "All right! All right!"

With some of the hands called down from aloft we got him between us and in some fashion carried him in to the top. Then a husky Dane shouldered him and carried him down on deck, where the mate met us.

"What th' devil's happened?" he shouted.

"Old Williams got aloft and he's all-in!"

The officer peered at the sodden bundle of humanity over the Dane's shoulders. "Well, I'll be scuppered!" he ejaculated. "The old Turk couldn't stay below when there was work to be done. Carry him in the fo'c'sle and I'll try and get a tot of rum for him."

We laid him in his bunk and he lay like one dead. His eyes were closed and he was breathing very, very faintly. There was the ominous blood trickle at the corners of his mouth. Old Williams would never leave his bunk alive. We could see that.

The mate came in with a tumbler of rum and we lifted up the old man's head and managed to force a little of the spirit between his lips. He gave a sigh and murmured, "Rum!" It was as though he were invoking the deity that had cursed his existence. We gave him one or two more sips and he opened his eyes and stared at us. The fire had gone from them now and they were dulled with the approach of death. Weakly, he motioned with his hand. "Rum!" he gasped, and we gave him another swallow.

He saw me leaning over him and grasped my wrist. Feebly drawing me nearer, I sensed his wishes and bent my head to his. "I'm slipping my cable, son. Goin' – out – with – th' – tide." He gasped and continued, "I – shipped – to – die – in – a – wind-bag–" another gasp, "in – deep – water." We gave him another sip. "My – last – job – weather – tops'l – yard – like a proper – sailor – man." His eyes closed and we thought he was gone, but he drew me to him again – very feebly, this time.

"Stitch me up . . . piece old sail . . . fisted many a time. Have – sails – make – neat – job. So . . . long!" He turned on his side with a consulsive shudder and went to meet the Great Pilot.

We dropped him over-side in the grey morning. The mate, who was a real sailor, acceded to his last request and furnished the sailmaker with a piece of old topsail canvas to fashion a shroud for the dead man. The Finnish sailmaker wielded his palm and needle with neatness and care as though the soul of the departed was standing-by to see that a proper seaman-like job was made in covering the dead clay.

And at eight bells, when the body lay on a grating placed on the rail, a rift appeared in the leaden clouds and a ray of sunshine threw a golden beam on the flag which covered the dead. It seemed as though the solar orb was paying a tribute to the passing out of that ancient sailorman and throwing a spot-light on the Red Ensign – the old red duster of Britain's Merchant Marine – under which he lay and under which he sailed . . . for sixty years.

Wilfred T. Grenfell

Born in Parkgate, Cheshire, England in 1865, Wilfred Thomason Grenfell attended Marlborough College in Wiltshire and then studied medicine in London. Deeply influenced by the American evangelist D.L. Moody, he embarked on a career of service in 1888, joining the National Mission to Deep-Sea Fisherman. In 1892, he was sent to Newfoundland and Labrador to assess the need for a medical mission. The following year, he established a hospital at Battle Harbour, Labrador. For the remainder of his life, he devoted himself to improving the lot of people in the scattered fishing communities of Newfoundland and Labrador. In 1912, the International Grenfell Association was formed. In addition to establishing hospitals, nursing stations, schools, and orphanages, the Association encouraged numerous economic ventures, including cooperatives and home industries. Grenfell promoted and financed his work through lectures and the writing of articles and books. Starting in 1895, he wrote more than forty volumes, many of which portray the lives of the seafarers of Labrador and Newfoundland. Among his works of sea fiction or non-fiction are *The Harvest of the Sea: A Tale of Both Sides of the Atlantic* (1905), *Down North on the Labrador*

(1912), and *Tales of the Labrador* (1916). One of his most memorable works is the autobiographical sea adventure *Adrift on an Ice-Pan* (1909). He died in Vermont in 1940.

"The Leading Light" appeared in Grenfell's *Labrador Days: Tales of the Sea Toilers* (1919). Like most of his stories, it is set on the Labrador coast, where a coastal voyage late in the year could be an extremely dangerous undertaking, and when the difference between life and death would often depend on a man's character.

The Leading Light

It was getting late in the year. The steep cliffs that everywhere flank the sides of the great bay were already hoary with snow. The big ponds were all "fast," and the fall deer hunt which follows the fishery was over. Most of the boats were hauled up, well out of reach of the "ballicater" ice. The stage fronts had been taken down till the next spring, to save them from being torn to pieces by the rising and falling floe. Everywhere "young slob," as we call the endless round pans growing from the center and covering the sea like the scales of a salmon, was making. But the people at the head of the bay were still waiting for those necessities of life, such as flour, molasses, and pork, which have to be imported as they are unable to provide them for themselves, and for which they must wait till the summer's voyage has been sent to market and sold to pay for them.

The responsibility of getting these supplies to them rested heavily on the shoulders of my good friend John Bourne, the only trader in the district. Women, children, whole families, were looking to him for those "things" which if he failed to furnish would mean such woeful consequences that he could not face the winter without at least a serious attempt to provide them.

In the harbour lay his schooner, a saucy little craft which he had purchased only a short while before. He knew her sea qualities; and as the ship tugged at her chains, moving to and fro on the swell, she kept a fine "swatch" of open water round her. Like some tethered animal, she seemed to be begging him to give her another run before Jack Frost gripped her in his chilly arms for months to come. The fact that he was a married man with hostages to fortune round his knees might have justified his conscience in not tempting the open sea at a time when frozen sheets and blocks choked with ice made it an open question if even a youngster ought to take the chances. But it happened that his "better half," like himself, had that "right stuff" in her which thinks of itself last, and her permission for the venture was never in question.

So Trader Bourne, being, like all our men, a sailor first and a landsman after, with his crew of the mate and a boy, and the handicap of a passenger, put to sea one fine afternoon in late November, his vessel loaded with good things for his necessitous friends "up along." He was encouraged by a light breeze which, though blowing out of the bay and there ahead for him, gave smooth water and a clear sky.

To those who would have persuaded him to linger for a fair wind he had cheerfully countered that the schooner had "two sides," meaning that she could hold her own in adversity, and could claw well to windward; besides, " 't will help to hold the Northern slob back" – that threatening spectre of our winters.

When darkness fell, however, very little progress had been made. The wind kept shifting against the schooner, and all hands could still make out the distant lights of home twinkling like tiny stars, apparently not more than a couple of miles under their lee.

"Shall us 'hard up,' and try it again at day's light?" suggested the mate. "If anything happens 't is a poor time of year to be out all night in a small craft."

But the skipper only shrugged his shoulders, aware that the mate was never a "snapper" seaman, being too much interested in gardens for his liking.

"It's only a mile or two to Beach Rock Cove. We'll make it on the next tack if the wind holds. 'T is a long leg and a short one, and we'll have a good chance then to make the Boiling Brooks to-morrow."

"Lee oh!" and, putting the helm up, the *Leading Light* was soon racing off into the increasing darkness towards the cliffs away on the opposite side of the bay.

The wind freshened as the evening advanced – the usual experience of our late fall nights. An hour went by, and as the wind was still rising, the flying jib was taken in. After this the captain sent the crew below for a "mug o' tea" while he took the first trick at the wheel.

Still the wind rose. The sea too was beginning to make, and the little craft started to fall to leeward too much to please the skipper. The men were again called, and together they reset all the head canvas. The *Leading Light* now answered better to her helm, and, heading up a point, reached well into the bay.

"Smooth water again before dawn," said the skipper in his endeavour to cheer the despondent mate, when once more they had gone aft. "Looks like clearing overhead. I reckon she'll be well along by daylight."

But the mate seemed "stun," and only grunted in return.

"You go down and finish supper, and then you can give me a spell at the wheel while I get my pipe lighted," continued the captain. Thereupon the other, nothing loath to have something to keep his mind diverted, was soon below, searching for consolation in a steaming mug, but failing to find it, in spite of the welcome contrast between the cosy warm cabin, and the darkness and driving spume on deck, lacking as he did, alas, the sea genius of our race.

"Watch on deck!" at length called Bourne; and a few minutes later, having entrusted the helm to the mate, he was lighting his pipe at the cabin fire. All of a sudden down, down, down went the lee floor of the cabin, and up, up, up went the weather, till it felt as if the little ship were really going over.

"What's up?" the skipper fairly yelled through the companion, as clinging and struggling his utmost he forced his way on deck, as soon as the vessel righted herself enough to make it possible. "Hard down! Hard down! Let her come up! Ease her! Ease her!" – and whether the puff of wind slackened or the mate lost hold of the wheel, he never has been able to tell, but she righted enough for a moment to let him get on the deck and rush forward to slack up the fore-sheet, bawling meanwhile through the darkness to the mate to keep her head up, as he himself tore and tugged at the rope.

The schooner, evidently well off the wind, yet with all her sheets hauled tight and clewed down, was literally flying ahead, but trying to dive right through the ponderous seas, instead of skimming over and laughing at them, as the captain well knew she ought to do. There was n't a second to lose pondering the problem as to why she would not come up and save herself. Difficult and dangerous as it was in the pitch dark with the deck slippery with ice, and the dizzy angle at which it stood, the only certain way to save the situation was to let go that sheet. Frantically he struggled with the rope, firmly clinched though it was round its cleats with the ice that had made upon it. Knowing how sensitive the vessel was and that she would answer to a half-spoke turn of the wheel, and utterly at a loss to understand her present stubbornness, he still kept calling to the helmsman, "Hard down! Hard down!" – only to receive again the growling answer, "Hard down it is. She's been hard down this long time."

It was all no good. Up, up came the weather rail under the terrific pressure of the wind. The fore-sheet was now already well under water, cleat and all, and the captain had just time to dash for the bulwark and hold on for dear life, when over went the stout little craft, sails, masts, and rigging, all disappearing beneath the waves. It seemed as if a minute more and she must surely vanish altogether, and all hands be lost almost within sight of their own homes.

Tumultous thoughts flooded the captain's mind as for one second he clung to the rail. Vain regrets were followed like lightning by a momentary resignation to fate. In the minds of most men hope would undoubtedly have perished right there. But Captain Bourne was made of better stuff. *"Nil desperandum"* is the

Englishman's soul; and soon he found himself crawling carefully hand over hand towards the after end of the vessel. Suddenly in the darkness he bumped into something soft and warm lying out on the quarter. It proved to be his passenger, resigned and mute, with no suggestion to offer and no spirit to do more than lie and perish miserably.

Still climbing along he could not help marking the absence of the mate and the boy from the rail, which standing out alone against the sky-line was occasionally visible. Doubtless they must have been washed overboard when the vessel turned turtle. There was some heavy ballast in the schooner besides the barrels of flour and other supplies in her hold. Her deck also was loaded with freight, and alas, the ship's boat was lashed down to the deck with strong gripes beneath a lot of it. Moreover, it was on the starboard side, and away down under water anyhow. Though every moment he was expecting the *Leading Light* to make her last long dive, his courage never for a second deserted him.

He remembered that there was a new boat on the counter aft which he was carrying with him for one of his dealers. She was not lashed either, except that her painter was fast to a stanchion. It was just possible that she might still be afloat, riding to the schooner as a sea anchor. Still clinging to the rail he peered and peered through the darkness, only to see the great white mainsail now and again gleam ghostlike in the dim light when the super-incumbent water foamed over it, as the *Leading Light* wallowed in the sullen seas. Then something dark rose against the sky away out beyond the peak end of the gaff – something black looming up on the crest of a mighty comber. An uncanny feeling crept over him. Yet what else could it be but the boat? But what could that

boat be doing out there? Fascinated, he kept glaring out in that direction. Yes, surely, there it flashed again across the sky-line. This
time he was satisfied that it was the boat, and that she was afloat
and partly protected by the breakwater formed by the schooner's
hull. She was riding splendidly. In an instant he recalled that he
had given her a new long painter; and that somehow she must
have been thrown clear when the ship turned over. Anyhow, she
was his only chance for life. Get her he must, and get her at once.
Every second spelt less chance of success. Any moment she might
break adrift or be dragged down by the sinking schooner. And
then came the horrible memory that she too had been stowed on
the lee side, and her painter also was under the mainsail and fastened now several feet below the surface. Even the sail itself was
under water, and the sea breaking in big rushes over it with every
comber that came along.

To get the boat was surely impossible. It only added to the
horror of the plight to perish there miserably of cold, thinking of
home and of the loved ones peacefully asleep so near, while the
way to them and safety lay only a few fathoms distant – torturing
him by its very nearness. For every now and then driving hard to
the end of her tether she would rush forward on a sea and appear
to be coming within his reach, only to mock him by drifting away
once more, like some relentless lady-love playing with his very
heartstrings. The rope under the sunken mainsail prevented her
from quite reaching him, and each time that she seemed coming to
his arms, she again darted beyond his grasp.

Whatever could be done must be done at once. Even now he
realized that the cold and wet were robbing him of his store of
strength. Could he possibly get out to where the boat was? There

might be one way, but there could be only one, and even that appeared a desperate and utterly futile venture. It was to find a footing somehow, to let go his vise-like grip of the rail, and leap out into the darkness across the black and fathomless gulf of water surging up between the hull and the vessel's main boom in the hope of landing in the belly of the sail; to be able to keep his balance and walk out breast high through the rushing water into the blackness beyond till he should reach the gaff; and so, clinging there, perchance catch the boat's painter as she ran in on a rebounding sea. There would be nothing to hold on to. The ever swirling water would upset a man walking in daylight on a level quayside. He would have nothing but a sunken, bellying piece of canvas to support him – a piece only, for the little leach rope leading from the clew to the peak marked a sharp edge which would spell the dividing line between life and death.

He had known men of courage; he had read of what Englishmen had done. But he had never suspected that in his own English blood could lie dormant that which makes heroes at all times. A hastily breathed prayer – his mind made up, letting go of the weather rail he commenced to lower himself to the wheel, hoping to get a footing there for the momentous spring that would in all probability land him in eternity. But even as he climbed a little farther aft to reach down to it, he found himself actually straddling the bodies of the missing mate and boy, who were cowering under the rail, supported by their feet against the steering-gear boxing.

Like a thunderclap the whole cause of the disaster burst upon his mind. The mate's feet planked against the spokes of the wheel suggested it. The helm was not hard down at all, and never had been. It was hard up all the time. He remembered, now that it was too late, that the mate had always steered hitherto with a tiller; that a wheel turns exactly the opposite way to the tiller; and that with every sail hauled tight, and the helm held hard over, the loyal little craft had been as literally murdered as if she had been torpedoed, and also their lives jeopardized through this man's folly. What was the good of him even now? There he lay like a log, as dumb as the man whom he had left clinging to the taffrail.

"What's to be done now?" he shouted, trying in vain to rouse the prostrate figure with his foot. "Rouse up! Rouse up, you fool!" he roared. "Are you going to die like a coward?" And letting himself down, he put his face close to that of the man who by his stupidity had brought them all to this terrible plight. But both the mate and boy seemed paralyzed. Not a word, not a moan could he get out of them. The help which they would have been was denied him. Once more he realized that if any one was to be saved, he and he alone must accomplish it. A momentary rest between two waves decided him. There was one half-second of trying to get his balance as he stood up, then came the plunge into the wild abyss, and he found himself floundering in the belly of the sail, struggling to keep his footing, but up to his waist in water. With a fierce sense of triumph that he was safely past the first danger, the yawning gulf between the rail and boom, he threw every grain of his remaining strength into the desperate task before him, and pushed out for the gaff that was lying on the surface of the sea, thirty feet away in the darkness. Even as he started a surging wave washed him off his feet, and again he found himself hopelessly wallowing in the water, but still in the great cauldron formed by the canvas.

How any human being could walk even the length of the sail under such circumstances he does not know any more than I do. But the impossible was accomplished, and somehow he was clinging at last like a limpet to the very end of the gaff, his legs already dangling over the fatal edge, and with nothing to keep him from the clutch of death beyond it but his grip of the floating spar. To this he must cling until the mocking boat should again come taut on the line and possibly run within his reach. The next second out of the darkness what seemed to the man in the sail a mountain of blackness rushed hissing at him from the chaos beyond, actually swept across him into the belly of the sail, and tore him from his rapidly weakening hold of the spar. With the energy of despair his hands went up and caught something, probably a bight in the now slackened painter. In a trice he was gripping the rail, and a second later he was safely inside the boat, and standing shaking himself like some great Newfoundland dog.

Even now a seemingly insuperable difficulty loomed ahead. He had no knife and was unable to let go the rope. Would he be able to take his comrades aboard, and would the schooner keep afloat and form a breastwork against the sea, or would it sink and, after all his battle, drag the boat and him down with it to perdition?

Philosophizing is no help at such a time. He would try for the other men. To leave them was unthinkable. Once more fortune was on his side. The oars were still in the boat, lashed firmly to the thwarts – a plan upon which he had always insisted. Watching his chance, and skillfully manœuvring, he succeeded in approaching the schooner stern first, when the cable just allowed him to touch the perpendicular deck. His shouts to the others had now quite a different ring. His words were commands, leaving no initiative to them. They realized also that their one and only chance for life lay in that boat; and returning hope lent them the courage which they had hitherto lacked. After a delay which seemed hours to the anxious captain at such a time, with skilful handling he had got all three aboard.

Once more he was face to face with the problem of the relentless rope, but again fortune proved to be on his side. It was the passenger, the useless, burdensome passenger, who now held the key to the situation. He had sensed the danger in a moment, and instantly handed the skipper a large clasp-knife. With it to free the boat from the wreck was but the work of a moment.

True, their position in a small open "rodney" in the middle of a dark, rough night in the North Atlantic was not exactly enviable, especially as the biting winter wind was freezing their clothing solid, and steadily sapping their small stock of remaining vitality.

Yet these men felt that they had crossed a gulf almost as wide as that between Dives and Lazarus. If they could live, they knew that the boat could, for the ice would not clog her enough to sink her before daylight, and as for the sea – well, as with the schooner, it was only a matter of handling their craft till the light came.

Meanwhile, though they did not then know it, they had drifted a very considerable way towards their own homes, so that, rowing in turn and constantly bailing out their boat they at length made the shore at the little village of Wild Bight, only a few miles away from their own. The good folk at once kindled fires, and bathed and chafed the half-frozen limbs and chilled bodies of the exhausted crew.

Now the one anxiety of all hands was to get home as quickly as possible for fear that some rumor of the disaster in the form of wreckage from the schooner might carry to their loved ones news of the accident, and lead them to be terrified over their apparent deaths. As soon as possible after dawn of day, the skipper started for home, having borrowed a small rodney, and the wind still keeping in the same quarter. To his intense surprise a large trap-boat manned by several men, seeing his little boat, hailed him loudly, and when on drawing near it was discovered who they were, proceeded to congratulate him heartily on his escape. Already the very thing that he had dreaded might happen must surely have occurred.

"How on earth did you know so soon?" he enquired, annoyed.

"As we came along before t' wind we saw what us took to be a dead whale. But her turned out to be a schooner upside down. We made out she were t' *Leading Light*, and feared you must all have been drowned, as there was no sign of any one on her upturned keel. So we were hurrying to your house to find out t' truth."

"Don't say a word about it, boys," said the skipper. "One of you take this skiff and row her back to Wild Bight, while I go with the others and try and tow in the wreck before the wind shifts. But be sure not to say anything about the business at home."

The wind still held fair, and by the aid of a stout line they were able, after again finding the vessel, to tow her into their own harbour and away to the very bottom of the Bight, where they stranded her at high water on the tiny beach under the high crags which shoulder out the ocean. By a clever system of pulleys and blocks from the trunks of trees in the clefts of the cliff she was hauled upright, and held while the water fell. Then the *Leading Light* was pumped out and refloated on the following tide. On examination, she was pronounced uninjured by her untimely adventure.

I owe it to John Bourne to say that the messenger forbidden to tell of the terrible experience told it to his own wife, and she told it – well, anyhow, the skipper's wife had heard of it before the *Leading Light* once more lay at anchor at her owner's wharf. Courage in a moment of danger, or to preserve life, is one thing. The courage that faces odds when the circumstances are prosaic and the decision deferred is a rarer quality. It was a real piece of courage which gave the little schooner another chance that fall to retrieve her reputation. She was permitted to deliver the goods against all odds, and what is more the captain's wife kissed him good-bye with a brave face when once again he let the foresail draw, and the *Leading Light* stood out to sea on her second and successful venture.

There is no doubt that when she went to bed in the ice that winter, she carried with her the good wishes and grateful thanks of many poor and lonely souls; and some have said that when they were walking round the head of the cove in which it was the habit of the little craft to hibernate, strange sounds like that of a purring cat were ofttimes wafted shoreward. "It is only the wind in her rigging," the skeptical explained; but a suspicion still lurks in some of our minds that the Eskimo are not so far from the truth in conceding souls to inanimate objects.

Archibald MacMechan

Archibald MacMechan was born in 1862 at Berlin (Kitchener), Ontario and was educated at the University of Toronto and Johns Hopkins University. In 1889 he became a professor of English at Dalhousie University in Halifax. One of Canada's leading literary scholars, MacMechan was also an accomplished popular historian and increasingly, during the last two decades of his life, devoted himself to the preservation of Nova Scotia's maritime heritage. In addition to collecting documents and artifacts, he produced a significant number of sea stories that were collected in three books: *Sagas of the Sea* (1923), *Old Province Tales* (1924), and *There Go the Ships* (1928). MacMechan's own love of the sea apparently began with an 1883 voyage to England on a cattleship. He died at Halifax in 1933. His best sea stories were later collected in *Tales of the Sea* (1947), edited by Thomas H. Raddall, with illustrations by Donald C. Mackay. An important study of MacMechan's life and work, Janet E. Baker's *Archibald MacMechan: Canadian Man of Letters*, appeared in 2000. Despite such attention, MacMechan remains an unjustly neglected figure in Canadian literary and intellectual history.

"Via London" was originally published in the Halifax *Sunday Leader* (July 16, 1922). Not long after, it was collected in *Sagas of the Sea*. Based primarily on Mather Byles DesBrisay's account of the *Industry* disaster in *History of the County of Lunenburg* (1895) and on a statement (now found at the National Archives of Canada in Ottawa) signed by the survivors in London, the story reveals MacMechan's considerable skills as a chronicler of maritime history. As a *New York Tribune* reviewer observed: "Mac-Mechan is clear-eyed and presents astonishing things with restraint, and grace and charm."

Via London

Nova Scotia has need of another Hakluyt to record the traffics
and discoveries, the disasters and the heroic deeds of the seafaring
provincials. For more than a century Nova Scotia keels ploughed
the seven seas in peace and war. Five thousand vessels, Howe
boasted, had been built in the province; and they carried the flag
to every port in the world. Once Nova Scotia had even a tiny navy
of her own. Privateering in three wars, mutinies, encounters with
pirates, dreary wrecks, incredible endurance, rescues from death
and destruction, crowd the record with moving incident. Many are
the tragedies of the sea. What the ordinary perils of navigation
may mean, what suffering seafaring folk may be called to undergo,
with what hearts they met their trials will be plain from this simple
tale of a little Nova Scotian coasting vessel. Because of the vessel's
irregular course, the tale has been entitled "Via London," but perhaps a better name would be "Angeline's Wedding Dress."

At seven o'clock on the morning of the 11th December, 1868, in the dim dawning of a winter's day, the schooner *Industry*, thirty-seven tons register, put out from the wharf behind Ronald Currie's store on the west bank of the beautiful La Have River. Below hatches she had stowed a cargo of dry and pickled fish, and on deck she carried a load of cord-wood for the Halifax market. Lewis Sponagle was captain; with Currie he was joint owner of vessel and lading. Three hands were sufficient for the needs of the small schooner; their names were Henry Legag, Henry Wolfe and Daniel Wambach. Besides, she carried two passengers, Lawrence Murphy of Lawrencetown, and a young girl belonging to La Have called Angeline Publicover, eighteen years of age, who was going to Halifax to buy her wedding dress. Her picture shows her to have been small and slight in figure, and fair in the face, with candid brown eyes, brown abundant hair, rosy cheeks, and kind smiling lips. It is a fine face. She would have made a comely bride. She could have had no forewarning of the many trials she was so soon called on to endure; nor could she have dreamed that she would prove a heroine in a dreadful extremity.

The day was cold with light westerly winds, which drove the *Industry* towards her port of destination, only fifty-four miles away. Perhaps no one remembered that Friday is not counted a lucky day for beginning a voyage. It was certainly ominous for the *Industry* and all on board. Using the earliest hours of daylight, she pushed out past Ironbound straight along the chord of the great double fold in the coastline made by Mahone and St. Margaret's Bays. In spite of the favourable wind, it was not a good sailing day. The westerly breeze was fickle, and the mild weather was merely the lull before the coming storm. It took the little schooner nearly seventeen hours to cover some forty miles, which means that she must have dawdled because the wind failed her. The short winter day passed; the black December night came on; the weather changed, and, with it, the fortunes of all on board the *Industry*.

About one o'clock in the morning of Saturday the 12th, they could see the light on Sambro Island, which for a century and more has been the beacon for all vessels approaching Halifax from the westward or the south. The light bore north north-east. The deceitful west wind which had so far favoured them now died away, and suddenly, with the very slightest warning, the storm swooped down upon them from the northeast, bringing the blinding snow with it and hiding the dim loomings of the land. Halifax harbour is beset with dangers. It is a wicked coast to beat up to in a black winter storm. Progress towards the port was impossible, so the helm was put over, and the *Industry* turned in her tracks to run for La Have. She went back faster than she came.

The veering of the wind must have been terribly sudden. Apparently the schooner was taken aback, for the first blast of the snowstorm split the foresail and made it useless. Henceforth the *Industry* was like a bird with one broken wing. This was only the first of the mishaps which befell the ill-starred vessel that dark night. At the same time the can of kerosene was spilled; the cabin lamp was never lit again; and it was no slight aggravation of their misery that more than half of every twenty-four hours must be spent in utter darkness.

In the double darkness of night and the thick driving snow, the *Industry* fled back to La Have before the north-east gale. It was still thick weather when Captain Sponagle judged that he was near Cross Island, the seamark sentinel before Lunenburg harbour, to which Lunenburg sailormen find their way back from the ends of the four oceans. The mouth of the La Have is just around the corner. Now the *Industry* was near home and safety, but once more her luck changed for the worse. The fierce gale suddenly chopped round to the northwest, driving the schooner back from her desired haven and out into the furious Atlantic. If her foresail had been intact, she might have been hove to, and so have ridden out the gale. In attempting to do so, the damaged sail was blown to rags. There was nothing for it but to dowse all sail and run before the storm. For three days and three nights the *Industry* scudded under bare poles straight out to sea. To take the dangerous weight off her, the deck-load of cord-wood was started overboard. In the darkness and confusion all available hands must have been working desperately to clear the deck. They were fighting for their lives, and in their haste another accident occurred. One of the two water-casks secured just forward of the main-mast went overboard with the cord-wood, and the other was so badly smashed that only two gallons of water was saved from it. This loss meant later intense suffering from thirst. The two gallons from the broken cask, and a kettleful of melted hail-stones gathered in a remnant of the foresail, was the whole water supply of seven persons for eighteen days. They were rationed to a wineglass apiece once in twenty-four hours. The last drop was finished on 27th December. Along with the deck-load went their only boat.

Never counting on more than the day's run to Halifax, the owners had not provisioned their little craft for such an unforeseen emergency as being blown out to sea. Food there was practically none. What little they had was spoiled by the salt water. For two weeks, from the 15th to the 29th of December, those seven persons sustained life on ten hard-tack. A tiny fragment of biscuit once in the twenty-four hours was the ration. On that and the thimbleful of water, they kept the life in their bodies for an endless fortnight. They dared not touch the salt fish in the hold, for fear of the thirst that would drive them mad. With fresh water they might have been able to cook the fish, though the stove was damaged in the hurly-burly of the first night. They found a few oats in a bag, and these they managed to parch on the top of the broken stove and eat. On Christmas Day they discovered one potato in the bilge. They divided it into seven portions, just and loyal in their misery.

"Our tongues were so swollen we could scarcely eat it."

On Tuesday the 15th they were able to do something besides hold on for dear life, as their frail little fabric raced the mountainous seas. In the turmoil of waters they saw another sail, an American fishing schooner, which ran down close enough to speak with the helpless *Industry*. The weather was too wild for the Americans to launch a boat with food and water, or to render any assistance whatever. For a few moments the two craft were near enough for Captain Sponagle to shout that he wanted his position and his course for Bermuda, and for the American skipper to shout back the necessary directions; then each went his way. Once more the crew got some canvas on the *Industry*, the jib and mainsail, both close-reefed no doubt, and, starving and parched with thirst, they held on for the Summer Islands. The gale was favourable; but they were not destined to reach the port they were headed for any more than Halifax. Tuesday was evidently their first breathing space. On this day Captain Sponagle took stock, collected his ten biscuits, and began rationing them out, as well as the precious two gallons of water. For three days the *Industry* held her course towards Bermuda, but the faint gleam of good fortune, the hope of reaching port, proved to be illusory.

Once more the cruel wind chopped round to the westward and blew a terrific gale. Evidently the little schooner was buffeted by a series of cyclonic storms. December 1868 was a particularly bad month all over the North Atlantic. Many were the wrecks and reports of disaster. Like the former, this gale lasted three days, "during which," says the original narrative, "we suffered severely." The severity of their sufferings is easy to realize. This last gale was the worst of all, and it grew wilder and wilder. The huge confused billows made a clean breach over the labouring schooner, tearing away her bulwarks, rails and stanchions, and flooding the tiny cabin. The force of the waves also wrenched the tarpaulin off the forward hatch and carried it away. To prevent the hold from being flooded and the vessel foundering there and then, the resourceful crew nailed over the hatch a cow-hide intended for the Halifax market; and it kept the water out. But with the prolonged and furious buffetings of wind and sea, the frame of the *Industry* was being racked apart, the seams opened, and she began to leak badly. To the sufferings from cold, hunger, thirst, was added the exhausting, endless labour of pumping to keep afloat.

"Our strength was fast failing, but we managed by dint of great exertion to pump the vessel."

To strain every muscle of arms and back at working a machine which hardly forces the water out as fast as it runs in and to know that your life depends upon your perseverance, is the toil of Sisyphus. If the water rose in the hold beyond a certain point, the vessel's reserve buoyancy would be gone, and, under the next swamping billow, she would go down like a stone. So these men laboured, hour after hour, day and night, on the reeling, wave-swept deck, toiling like slaves, with a few crumbs of biscuit, and a wine-glass of water to sustain their strengths.

Christmas Day with its happy memories, brought increase of misery to all on board the *Industry*. Their Christmas dinner was the solitary raw potato divided into seven portions, which they could scarcely eat. Christmas night was remembered for its terrors; it was a night of despair. Work at the pump was abandoned as useless. There was no one at the tiller; hope was gone. All seven were huddled together in the inky darkness of the little cabin. Overhead tons of water crashed upon the roof as the unguided *Industry* pitched and rolled and wallowed in the giant billows. There was nothing to do but hold on and wait for the inevitable end. The schooner might go down at any moment.

What was done in that cabin is best told in the words of a survivor.

"We were nearly exhausted with hunger and exposure and our thirst was dreadful, and expecting every moment to be our last we united in prayer to the Almighty and shook hands with each other, as we thought, for the last time. Most of the men gave way to tears, but our only female passenger cheered us with the hope that our prayers were answered, and we were strengthened again to pump the ship."

"Extremity is the trier of spirits," says Shakespeare. "Hope," says Chesterton wisely, "is the power of being cheerful in circumstances which we know to be desperate. . . . The virtue of hope exists only in earthquake and eclipse. . . . For practical purposes it is at the hopeless moment that we require the hopeful man. . . .

Exactly at the instant when hope ceases to be reasonable it begins to be useful."

These words fit the situation to a nicety. It is no wonder that men, weakened by a fortnight of exposure, starvation, thirst and exhausting labour, should shed hysterical tears; nor is it their shame. But the spirit of the "female passenger" did not break or bend. In the black darkness of that little cabin, the courage and hope of a mere girl shone like a star. Angeline Publicover cheered the despairing men by her faith in the mercy of God, and they were "strengthened" to resume their Sisyphean labours. On board the *Industry* the last morsel of food was eaten, the last drop of water drunk, when rescue came. All these weary days driving hither and thither in mid-Atlantic, another vessel was sailing to cross her track. The predestined meeting came to pass on 29th December.

The Coalfleets of Hantsport were a typical family of Nova Scotia mariners. Once a nameless baby drifted ashore from the wreckage of a collier on the coast. The boy lived, and from these circumstances was given the name Coalfleet, meet origin for a seafaring clan. From him was descended Hiram Coalfleet, one of six brothers, all of whom followed the sea. He was a master mariner, honourable, looked up to, and a skilful navigator. In command of the Nova Scotia barque *Providence* of four hundred and eighty tons, he was now on his way from Philadelphia to London with a cargo of kerosene. His brother Abel sailed with him as chief mate.

His vessel got her name in a curious way. She was built in the beautiful little town of Canning by the well-known firm of Bigelow. When she stood almost complete on the ways with a little schooner beside her, the master builder decided that as the timbers were ready, the schooner should be launched that day. So it was done, and she floated safely into the narrow tidal river Pereau. That very afternoon a fire broke out which swept the whole village, but it stopped short at the barque's hull; the flames scorched her sides. If the schooner had remained on the ways, both vessels must have been burned. Hence the schooner was christened *Escape*, and the barque *Providence*. Now the *Providence* was to earn her name a second time.

Seven hundred miles east of Nova Scotia, she sighted a vessel, as the expressive language of the sea puts it, "in distress." That so small a craft should be so far from land implied accident, and the wave-swept deck and the jagged fragments of bulwarks would tell their own tale. The *Providence* bore down on the schooner under storm canvas, lay to, and tried to launch her long-boat. It was still blowing a gale with a heavy sea running, and getting the big heavy boat over the side into the sea was no easy task. After several attempts, it was smashed and lost. The only other boat on board was too small to live in such a sea. But Captain Coalfleet was not at the end of his resources. He tried another means of rescue which put his own ship in peril, which called for most skilful handling of her, and which would fail but for cool, swift, decisive action. He manœuvred his big barque to windward of the little coaster, backed his topsail, and drifted down on the *Industry* broadside on. He must have calculated his distance to a nicety, and he must have had a well-disciplined crew; no lubbers or wharf-rats stood by the sheets and braces that December day. He was risking his own ship with all on board, for collision was inevitable; his part was to minimize the shock of contact. As the two vessels swung crashing together, the main-yard of the *Providence* fouled the rigging of the *Industry*. Nimble as a cat, Abel Coalfleet ran up on the main-yard, lay out along it, and, with a line in his hand, probably the clue-garnet, let himself down swiftly on the tossing deck of the schooner. Any passenger on an ocean steamer who has ever watched the antics of the pilot's boat alongside in comparatively smooth water, can form some conception of the way two vessels rolling, tossing, pitching, grinding together would behave in a midwinter Atlantic storm. Abel Coalfleet, balancing on the yard-arm, which pointed in the sky one moment, and, the next, almost dipped in the waves, makes the acrobatics of the circus and moving pictures look silly. He must have been as cool-headed as he was brave and strong and nimble. He might have lost his hold and been flung into the sea, or entangled in the cordage, or crushed between the grinding hulls. As he dropped to the reeling, wave-swept schooner's deck, he fastened a line to the one woman on board, who was speedily hauled up the side of the *Providence*. The six men were also swiftly pulled on board by means of ropes the crew flung to them, with Abel Coalfleet always aiding. Then he slashed the stay which held the yard-arm of the *Providence* fettered, and swarmed up the barque's side like the people he had saved; the backed topsail swung round promptly, and the *Providence*, having sustained "much damage," was once more put on her course for London. The rescue could only have taken a few minutes; it was effected "most expeditiously" say the rescued, in a smart and seaman-like manner. The collision gave the *coup de grâce* to the battered little coaster. Three-quarters of an hour later, she disappeared beneath the stormy Atlantic with her cargo of dry and pickled fish, her broken stove, and the cow-skin on the fore-hatch. The *Providence* had come up just in time.

Of course, saving life at sea is more or less a habit with sailors, all in the day's work, and nothing to call for remark. A dry, matter-of-fact entry in the log of the *Providence* would close the incident. But this rescue was exceptionally hazardous and brilliant. The skill of Captain Hiram in handling his big ship was equaled by the way Abel seconded him. Sponagle, with a sailor's appreciation, records that he "gallantly hazarded his life to save ours." Gallant is the word.

The rescued seven considered their preservation while in the *Industry* "perfectly miraculous, and the manner in which we were relieved almost as wonderful." But they were in the last stages of exhaustion, with bodies wasted by nearly three weeks of starvation, and with tongues so swollen that they could hardly speak. All on board were most kind to the castaways, but they still had many hardships to undergo. Their proper place was a hospital ward with careful nursing and nutritious food until their sorely-tried bodies recovered their tone. But the resources of a Nova Scotia barque in the sixties were limited; she would carry only coarse food to meet the bare necessities. Moreover the taste of kerosene had got into the food and water, and produced painful sickness. It was not until three weeks after their rescue, on 20th January, 1869, that they reached London, weak, utterly destitute, but thankful to God for His mercy that they were alive.

From London they were forwarded to Liverpool by kind friends, whence they returned to Halifax by the Inman Line steamer *Etna*. Angeline Publicover was particularly well treated by the ladies on board, who dressed her "like a queen." So at length they reached the port they set out for on 12th February in a varied and circuitous passage of sixty-one days. The newly organized Dominion of Canada paid the traveling expenses of these shipwrecked Nova Scotians. The Halifax papers showed no interest in the event; they did not interview the castaways, print their "story" or their pictures. Such adventures and exploits were too common. The shipping news occupied but small space in the local journals and is to be found under the heading "Reports, Disasters, etc." The "etc." is eloquent. In the sixties was the heyday of Nova Scotia shipping. The great industry of the province was reaching its peak of prosperity. So six or seven lines, not quite accurate, of unemotional minion type told this tale of heroism in the "Reports, Disasters, etc." column, and that was the end of it. At home, the rescued men were welcomed as if risen from the dead.

The conduct of the Coalfleets was brought to the notice of the governor-general, and in due time Hiram was presented with a gold watch and Abel with a pair of binoculars suitably inscribed. The watch must have been lost, with other possessions, when the ironically christened *Happy Home* was wrecked on the Trinity ledges, 3rd January, 1881. When she fell over and sank, all hands got into the mizzen rigging. His wife and nine-year-old daughter Mary died beside Captain Coalfleet that winter night, and his legs were frozen to the knees.

Of the forgotten heroine of the *Industry*, Angeline Publicover, it is recorded that she never bought her wedding dress. In *Aes Triplex* Stevenson asks, "What woman could be lured into marriage, so much more dangerous than the wildest sea?" Angeline had had her experience of the wildest sea. She was a good girl and a brave girl. Long-drawn suffering and deadly peril only revealed the native strength of a character which must be called heroic.

cArthur Hunt Chute

Arthur Hunt Chute was born at Stillman Valley, Illinois in 1888 and grew up in Halifax and Wolfville. A graduate of Acadia College, he later studied at Newton Theological Institution and Edinburgh University. However, his studies were interrupted in 1913 when he volunteered to fight in the Second Balkan War. Following his graduation from the Newton Theological Institution in 1914, he volunteered again for military service, participating in the American occupation of Veracruz, Mexico. Later that year, he joined the Canadian army, serving overseas during the First World War until 1917, when he was invalided home. After his recovery, Chute began lecturing and publishing in the United States about the Allied war effort. His war-related articles were eventually collected in *The Real Front* (1918). At the end of the war, Chute decided to commit himself to journalism, rather than to the ministry. Dividing his time between Wolfville, Bermuda, and New York, he specialized in economic subjects and was soon contributing to a wide variety of British, American, and Canadian periodicals and newspapers. In addition to his non-fiction, Chute wrote a large body of sea fiction that appeared in magazines such as *Argosy*, *Sea Stories*, and *American Boy*. Three of his serialized novels were later published in book form: *The Mutiny of the Flying Spray* (1927), *Far Gold* (1927), and *The Crested Seas* (1928). Chute's promising literary career was cut short in 1929, when he died in a plane crash in Lake Manitoba, near Reykjavik.

Chute is represented by two stories, "The Hell Driver" and "The Avenger." "The Hell Driver," which first appeared in *Argosy All-Story Weekly* (March 24, 1923), is one of several tales that he wrote about Red Alec Campbell, a bold and profane master from Judique. "The Avenger" is taken from *Sea Stories* (December 1925) and features another Judique fisherman, Wild Archie MacEacheren. It is a tale in which vengeance takes an unexpected form. Both stories reveal Chute's profound admiration for defiant men of action. Although not as experienced a seafarer as most of his heroes, Chute did own an Able Seaman's certificate, which, according to his father, "he prized more than if it were a parchment from some great school of learning."

The Hell Driver

In their office overlooking Gloucester Harbor sat John Mystic, John Startling, and John Bluejacket – John MacDonalds all, but differentiated by the names of vessels they had formerly commanded. With them was their junior partner, Eddie Campbell.

It was the hour when the old timers lit their pipes and let their fancies roam. Always those fancies turned toward Judique, their boyhood home, on the north shore of Cape Breton, a section inhabited by Canadian Highlanders who still spoke the Gaelic of the Western Isles. Judique was a land of long ago, and these three, looking backward, beheld it through eyes of fond enchantment.

This afternoon the talk turned to what Eddie Campbell regarded as daring sailing on the part of some of the MacDonald captains.

Word had come of one of their schooners jumping a bar on the gulf shore of Prince Edward Island to escape foundering in a hurricane.

"That fellow must have been a nervy skipper," ventured the new partner in admiration.

"A nervy nothing," exclaimed John Startling with contempt. "We've got no high line devils in our fleets these days. If ye want a true blue hell driver, ye should go down north and see the white ships of Judique. Aye, we've had some dogs down there. But a son of Diarmuid of yer ain ilk was the king of 'em all."

"Who's that?" inquired Eddie.

"Captain Red Alec Campbell, of the *Pass of Balmaha*."

With voice from wistful memory, John Startling told the tale of the greatest shiphandler that ever came out of Judique.

Red Alec was the bonnie dog of a fleet where they could all crack on the dimty. It was a love affair that helped him on in his wild career. The Campbell and one Ronald Donn were both smitten on a lass named Mary MacLeod. She liked the Campbell best, but her folks prevailed upon her to take the more sober, steady Ronald Donn, after which the disappointed lover went to hell with a bang. Whenever Red Alec saw Ronald Donn with his lost sweetheart he was smitten with fits of long-continued madness. When these fits were on him he would do the desperate things that became the talk of the north shore ports.

No ordinary shipowner would have given him a vessel, but Charles P. Maclehose, owner of the white ships of Judique, was no ordinary shipowner. Maclehose was a bluff Glasgow Scotchman, past the prime of life, who enjoyed owning speedy, handsome vessels. In truth he was the magnate of Cape Breton; the steel works, the coal mines and the Caledonia fisheries all served to swell his income. The white fleet was his one extravagance.

He was wont to exclaim: "Some that have the money keep fast women, some keep fast horses; I keep fast ships."

Far from being fancy racing machines, his vessels were built to stand any amount of driving and hard weather. He cared for nothing but the best in design and construction, and fitted them with spare gear, stores and provisions in the most generous scale. Then he turned them over to masters and crews from Judique for service on the Banks. Some would have it that the chief was crazy, the way he made a sport of the fishing business, but he could afford to pay for his whims.

Red Alec Campbell's madness, with other owners a vice, with Maclehose was a virtue. For him torn canvas and split spars were incidentals to a record run.

It was a custom which the chief had instituted to have a race among his fleet every year to the Western Bank at the opening up of the fishing season.

The queen of his beautiful white schooners had always been named the *Pass of Balmaha*. There had been three of that name, the first two having run their bows under from foolhardy sail carrying. The *Pass of Balmaha*, third, the last and finest vessel, had experienced bad luck under Captain Roary MacDonald. Just before the big race that year the chief replaced Captain Roary by Captain Alec Campbell.

The dark horse for the coming contest was none other than the Campbell's late rival in love, Ronald Donn, who with the *Royal Stuart* had already shown his wake to the queen of the fleet.

Just before the event odds were pretty even. The heavy gamblers backed the *Pass of Balmaha*, while the more conservative shook their heads and put their money on the *Royal Stuart*.

Among the crew of the *Pass of Balmaha* were some of the hardest lads out of Judique, including wild Archie MacEacheren, the champion fighter, his brother Allan, Little Roary the Piper, and a dozen others. They were a gang that would follow their skipper to the death, all except Arch Campbell, whose heart was too weak for the company he kept.

When the day of the race came it was what the bloods had prayed for – a day with a wind to blow the barn over the house.

The fleet was due to sail from MacNair's at four in the afternoon. Just before that time at the wharves along the Sunnyside Bend there was a merry babel – the *clomp, clomp, clomp* of the windlass pawl, the Jacobite songs of the Highland crews, the hum of the running gear, reeving through the blocks, and the music of the straining sheaves to last long pulls on sheets and halyards.

The *Pass of Balmaha* was the first to push her nose into the strait. Half a gale was blowing from the northeast. To show his respect for the weather Red Alec immediately began to shake out his topsails.

As the graceful schooner gathered headway the onlookers agreed that they had never seen a vessel which in passing through the water disturbed it less. Hardly a ripple curled at the cut-water, nor did the sea break at any place along her sides. She left a wake as straight as an arrow. Then getting the wind with increasing speed, she began to raise the arc of her forefoot gently to meet the coming swell.

The *Royal Stuart* under four lowers was the second to cat her anchor and lie down in the wake of Red Alec, who was already standing back from the opposite shore.

Soon the strait was alive with the snowy wings, tearing back and forth in the narrow channel.

At high tide, which occurred that afternoon at four, the vessels were due to cross the line. Two blasts of the foundry whistle was the five-minute warning. One blast at the hour was the signal for the start.

It was now nearly high water, and the tide would soon be running ebb. Most of the fleet were bunched together on the offshore. But Red Alec, the canny fox, was far out of the crowd well up to windward. In the jockeying for position his strategy had gained the first advantage.

As the two blasts of the warning whistle sounded, Red Alec emerged from the companion, an unearthly pallor upon his face, a fiendish hatred glinting in his eye. He had been drinking Demerara rum below. Under the influence of liquor he kept his head, but, seized with a strange madness, he began to regard the sea as his bitterest foe.

Taking the wheel from Wild Archie, the skipper sent his eye up along the bellying canvas, while the vessel responded to his touch like a thoroughbred to the hand of a master.

"What's the record for the run to the Western Ground?" he inquired as he trimmed his wheel.

"Cap'n Hooty Mac Askill in *Pass of Balmaha*, first, thirteen hours; Cap'n John Cameron in *Pass of Balmaha*, second, eleven hours," answered Wild Archie.

"All right; fer us it's Western Ground or hell in ten hours."

With a final swing he threw the vessel into the course for the take off, bellowing as he did so: "Sheet home yer foretops'l and set yer stays'l."

Having made his last gauging of time and distance, with the daring of a born cavalry leader he shot like a rocket straight down upon the starting line. Ten seconds after the whistle the *Pass of Balmaha* flashed across the line, her lee side buried in a smother of foam.

The *Royal Stuart*, the *Lochaber*, the *Bonnie Prince Charlie*, the *Glengarry*, the *Airlie*, the *Keppoch* and the *Dundee*, in order named, came storming after.

Bowling along wing and wing through the straits with all sail drawing except the jibs, the white fleet sped away before the wind at a tremendous clip.

An hour later the *Pass of Balmaha*, pressed close by the *Royal Stuart*, shot out of the protecting straits into Chedabucto Bay, where she encountered a nasty rolling sea upon her port quarter. With every stitch cracked on she began to roll into it like a drunkard.

Red Alec lost no time preparing for bad weather. The dories nested in the waist were turned bottom up and made doubly secure. Extra lashings were put on spare spars and gear.

At six o'clock that evening they raised Cranberry Light. By this time the weather was looking wilder and the glass had begun to fall.

With a growing gale offshore the redoubtable skipper respected the prospects enough to order: "Put the tops'l in gaskets and stow away yer stays'l."

Before reaching Cranberry Island all hands were ordered to put a single reef in the great mainsail.

The skipper set his course on the inside channel, tearing through the shipping of Canso Harbor, grazing fishermen and stormstaid coasters, who looked after him aghast racing thus before a rising gale.

For a short time in the lee of the mainland the crew had a breathing space, while they tussled with reef points of the slotting mainsail. Then around by Glasgow Head, at the farther end of the harbor, they struck the full force of the open sea.

"Here comes the Atlantic," yelled Wild Archie, who had taken his place beside the skipper at the wheel. Through the dangerous waters just off of Glasgow Head, with the lead going, the *Pass of Balmaha* raced hell for leather.

Fishermen beating in against the storm looked askance at the great Judiquer outbound into the smother of the howling night.

After a short turn at the wheel Wild Archie came gasping into the forecastle, exclaiming: "Talk about yer stunts! This auld lass is sure acting now; this minute she's waltzin' on her bowsprit, the next standin' on her counter."

"D'ye think Red Alec 'll make it in ten hours?"

"Sure thing he'll make it. We may take our trick at the wheel an' be relieved, but the skipper 'll stand by up there till he's clubbed his mud hook to the lee o' west point lights."

This conversation was cut short by a voice shouting: "Hi, there, all hands rouse out quick! Here's ice close aboard!"

Tearing along under single-reefed mainsail, whole foresail, and jib with the bonnet out, all the sail she could carry, it needed no second alarm. Meeting floating ice at such speed meant that if the vessel struck her bows would be crushed like eggshell.

There was no time to wait for oilskins or jackets. Bareheaded, in shirt sleeves, all hands came rushing up into the freezing night. A lookout jumped into the rigging, and for nearly an hour clung there directing the captain how to steer.

Fortunately it was bright moonlight. Hundreds of isolated cakes appeared before the ship. Realizing the magnitude of the peril, Red Alec yelled: "Take in the fores'l."

This order none were loath to obey. Indeed, the crew would gladly have stripped off every stitch. But it was heartbreaking enough for the skipper to give up the foresail.

At reduced speed he threaded his way through the floating ice pans. After fifty minutes of nerve-racking vigilance they emerged into open water.

"Is she all clear ahead?"

"All clear ahead!" came back from the lookout.

"All right, then, up again with the fores'l."

Very gingerly the hands began to obey.

"Come on now, put some snap into it an' get that sail aloft."

Soon the *Pass of Balmaha* was staggering under an incredible pressure of canvas. With her sheets well off she went rushing through the darkness like some black-winged specter.

As if this were not enough for a driving gale, Red Alec, who had been haunted by thoughts of Ronald Donn during the time lost in the ice field, sang out: "Get the stays'l out and bend it on her."

A muttered protest came from the horrified crew.

"It's suicide."

"It's murder."

"It's tempting Providence too far."

Such ejaculations were immediately smothered. "Get that stays'l up, I tell ye!"

Red Alec was a man master as well as a shipmaster. Some men were finally pausing, as if the job were complete, when the whiplash tongue urged them on.

"Break yer backs on that halyard till she's flat as a board."

Over and over went the lee rail till every roll nigh stopped the heartbeat. While all hands were still on deck the skipper addressed them from the wheel:

"Now, then, ye lads frae below what got caught napping, get into yer oilskins and stay in 'em. Don't forget that this here hooker's fightin' sudden death. That means every mother's son o' ye on board is fightin', too. Watch on and watch off. Keep oiled up, ready to jump fer yer lives at every call. Those on deck stand by every minute to tend sheets, fer we're goin' to be on our berth in ten hours, or we're goin' to be in hell."

Once Allan MacEacheren, beside the master, suggested: "That stays'l's too much sail, ain't it, skip?"

"I know it is, but she's up hard, and no one this side of eternity 'll bring her down. Not a rag o' canvas 'll come off frae now on unless it's ripped off wi' the hand o' God 'lmighty."

At the wheel, sometimes buried to the waist in water, Red Alec was fighting the seas in earnest. With cool-headed daring, not too bold and not too cautious, he gauged his chances to the utmost and ventured always to that very limit.

Every minute he kept his watch on deck, fighting to gain every last ounce of advantage. Under single reeved, double reeved, close reefed mainsail, reefs in and reefs out, with watchful eye he made use of every lull and slant to drive his vessel across the long, fierce, swooping combers.

Such driving was too much for Arch Campbell.

"He'll crack the sticks out of her or run her bow clear under," he muttered, his fingers itching to ease the sheets.

As he kept up his ominous muttering, Little Roary exclaimed: "Should 'ave left the likes of 'im at home. He'll be our Jonah yet."

About an hour after clearing the ice the *Pass of Balmaha*, caught unawares by a sudden squall, was thrown completely on her beam ends. A Niagara of water went pouring down the forehatch. The watch below thought that the end had come, but before they had time to gather their wits through her own momentum the racing vessel righted herself and began to come up.

As the wind struck into her sails she started again with a rush and drew herself out from beneath the seas that swept her from the mainmast aft.

Like souls redeemed from the bottomless pit, those below came bursting through the scuttle, breathing with thankful gasps the fresh keen air, gazing with gratitude upon the moon and stars.

More than one deep-souled Highlander sent up his prayer of thanks to Mary, who had miraculously saved them, and to St. Michael, the guardian and patron of those upon the sea.

But if the rest of his crew were devoutly thankful, no such emotion welled up in the rum-fired heart of Red Alec. Hearing a Gaelic "Ave" muttered by one of the MacEacherens set him into an insensate rage.

"No Mary and no Michael will save ye aboard this hooded hooker. It's only yer two fists and the leapin' lightnin' in yer heels that can preserve for ye the breath o' life that's in yer nostrils.

"If it's devotions yer wantin' one gang o' ye can take it out in sweat and elbow grease on yer prayer handles cleaning up that mess along the waist. The other gang can haul for the salvation of yer souls on them sheets and halyards.

"Now, there, jump my bullies and don't forget that ye're Judique Men."

Such was the potency of the man-driving skipper that his passion was soon flaming up throughout his crew, while his vessel rode again serene.

Hove to under double-reefed foresail, the watch of a coaster saw far off in the fitful moonlight, a soaring white ship, tearing on before the gales, like some archangel of the tempest.

While the watch of the coaster looked aghast they beheld a foretopsail broken out and added to the billowy mass of canvas.

"Howling Lucifer!" exclaimed a deckhand. "Did ye ever see the likes o' that before, goin' by in a full gale with every stitch cracked on, an' summer kites to boot! Do I see right, or am I dreaming? Is that real timber and canvas, or is it the Flying Dutchman?"

"That's real timber and canvas," answered the coaster's captain, "but it ain't goin' to be real much longer. That's one o' them crazy, wild-driving, hell-roaring ships from Judique, full o' Cape Breton Jacobites and Demerara rum. Oh, my Lord! Oh, my Lord! But ain't they drunk!"

Yes, drunk they were, with a wine undreamed of to that breed upon the coaster's deck.

The Viking horde that raped the mouth of the Western Isles did not take all. They left behind that Viking soul, which now lived on in Red Alec and his Highland shipmates. No wonder the ground hogs on a wallowing coaster called them "drunk." What could they understand? But across the centuries a crew of Norsemen would have hailed them as blood brothers from the stormy coasts of Skye.

In the wild tearing flight even the passage of time seemed to fade. But Red Alec did not forget. Finally he sang out.

"Run down into the cabin, one of ye, and tell me what's the hour o' night."

"Eleven o'clock," came back the answer.

"Eleven," he repeated, "seven hours, and by the log ninety-five miles. Thirty yet to go. Yea, we'll make it in ten hours, and beat every record of the Hielan fleet. Aye, lads, but am I not a dog and a bonnie driver? I'll show – "

The Highlanders' vainglorious song was suddenly cut short by a *whir – rupp – bang!*

The great staysail, torn to tatters, flapped and slatted away to leeward. This was followed by another long, ripping tear and a booming crack as the foretopsail and foretopmast carried away together.

Almost instantaneously there came a shout of dismay from Wild Archie, who had been hanging on to the after rail.

Intent only on that before, no one had heeded what might be aft or on the quarter. It was a casual glance which revealed with startling suddenness the fact that another schooner was pressing them close, a half a mile to windward.

All hands started in surprise while the skipper, with far-seeing eye, cried out:

"My God, if that there ain't Ronald Donn!"

"That looks bad," commented Wild Archie. "Jest after our foretopmast carried away! A pretty mess yon 'll put us into when we round the nor'wes' bar, and start our thrash to windward."

"Yes, it do look bad, but I've a trick that 'll settle wi' Ronald Donn."

On the run from MacNair's fortune had favored the *Royal Stuart*. When Red Alec split tacks and went through Canso Harbor Ronald Donn held his course, steering straight for sea. Thus he escaped the delaying ice. With foretopmast intact he was obviously in better condition for the windward work of the last lap.

Gradually, but none the less surely, Ronald Donn closed down upon the queen of the fleet. For some time both vessels had been taking soundings and each had its lookout aloft to pick up the first flash of the west point light of Sable Island.

Simultaneously there came the cry:

"Light on the starboard bow!"

With that cry Ronald Donn sang out: "Ready about, hard a lee!"

The next minute steering south-southeast with wind aft, he came bearing down upon Red Alec.

Every hand aboard the *Pass of Balmaha* stood ready waiting for the same order. A murderous light, glinted in the eye of the undefeated smuggling captain, but not a word escaped him.

The *Pass of Balmaha* had the right of way. But why did she continue on her old course southeast when every second now she should be driving it south-southeast to round the dreadful bar?

"Ain't ye goin' to come about now, skipper?" inquired Allan MacEacheren.

"Hold her to her auld course," snapped the skipper.

"He's going to drown us all to gain his vengeance over Ronald Donn," muttered Arch Campbell in despair.

Like mad bulls charging for a finish the two great racing schooners bore down upon each other. Red Alec held to his purpose with the determination of grim death, while Ronald Donn, just as sure that he would round to jibe, continued on a course which brought him fair across the other's bows.

Nearer and nearer the distance closed between the opposing captains, with the crews of each pleading in vain to cease their fatal obstinacy. When the impending crash was imminent it dawned upon the unwilling brain of Ronald Donn that his rival proposed holding to his suicidal purpose. Reluctantly he gave the order that brought his vessel's head up to the wind, with an abruptness that buried his lee rail, and threatened to splinter his spars. At the same time the *Pass of Balmaha* went forging onward. With vast relief the respective crews watched as they swiftly drew asunder.

After he had put nearly a mile between himself and Ronald Donn, Red Alec shouted:

"Douse the lights!"

The intended strategy flashed upon his shipmates and the order was carried out with a rush.

Looking backward Ronald Donn saw the lights of his rival suddenly swallowed up in darkness.

"God be about us! The *Pass of Balmaha* has gone under!" he exclaimed aghast. "They might 'a' kenned it the way they was heading. That Red Alec was mad if ever a man was. No use to put about, though. It would only be death for us, too, if we ventured too close to that uncanny shoal."

For twenty miles to the westward of Sable Island there extended a sandy bar, known as the graveyard of the North Atlantic. It was a spot reeking with wrecks. Straight into the teeth of this most dreaded menace the *Pass of Balmaha* went tearing with her lights extinguished.

The roar of breakers that could be heard for many miles boomed about the racing schooner. The sounding lead was kept going continually. With increasing shallowness, the seas were piling up to incredible heights while the breath of the gale lashed the night with foaming spindrift.

Such gambling with death was too much for Arch Campbell. Coming up to the wheel he began to implore the skipper to head off.

"She'll never live in that!" he almost screamed.

At the first note of fear the skipper cut him short. Striving for his very existence he was in no mood to brook remonstrance.

"Git the hell out o' me sight!"

Arch Campbell stood for a moment, irresolute, when the boot of a giant, Wild Archie, caught him fair and sent him headlong down the companion.

With the chicken heart removed, all the rest were one with the captain, ready with him to venture to the end.

Red Alec, during one of his rum-running expeditions, had been chased by a government cruiser into this self-same northeast bar. Rather than capture he risked running aground. By that strange fortune that sometimes guards the desperate he tripped upon a navigable channel and safely made the passage through. Toward this veritable leap in the dark he once more set his hazardous course.

"We're shaving corners," he exclaimed. "But I ken a ticklish passage that 'll put us over."

They were tearing on at a twelve knot clip, with a living gale abeam.

"By the deep six," came the man at the sounding.

"What's coming next, skipper?" inquired Allan MacEacheren.

"Five fathoms is coming next," answered the other, and almost simultaneously a voice shrieked: "By the mark five!"

Out of respect for that shrieking tone Red Alec spat to windward with supreme disdain.

Arch Campbell, respectful and subdued, but still in agonizing terror emerged trembling from below. The sight that greeted him was awe-inspiring and sublime. The full moon was flooding with its silver light the gale-lashed seas. Above the shallow bar great, shining, shimmering combers went soaring skyward, filling the night with the deep diapason of their roar. In the trough of the waves were valleys of inky blackness, while aloft the breaking crests shone like snowy, glistening peaks.

In this grand panorama Arch Campbell beheld only a yawning ocean graveyard.

"Ye can't go through there," he screamed, "I looked at the chart below. Ye've only five fathoms, then four, then three, then two. How can a vessel drawing fifteen feet go over a bar that at high tide gives only twelve feet of water?"

"Ye looked at the chart, did ye," taunted Red Alec, "Well, ye're sailin' wi' a skipper that kens more about these waters than any chart."

Momentarily Arch Campbell found reassurance in this note of bravado. Then another hail from forward renewed his panic.

"By the mark four."

His heart beat paused at that last call. Four fathoms, shoaling every minute and driving toward the most ominous bar on the northern seas!

Ahead, astern, on every quarter nothing could be seen but mountains of tumbling water. But over all Red Alec caught the intermittent flashes of the revolving light. By that flash he set his course.

Currents changeable and unchartable were forever working ruin to old landmarks and old soundings. A westward sweep of the Arctic current varying with the wind tore across the snary floor, carving out amid its shifting shoals a deep channel, whose wild environment was enough to daunt the most intrepid.

Arch Campbell was paralyzed with terror. Jumping a bar was too much for his cautious nature. But all the rest, like the skipper, were reckless gamblers, reckless alike with life or death.

The spirit of Red Alec was rising with the rising odds. As though it were a human being, he continued a dance of scorn in the face of his arch enemy, the sea.

"Come on and do your damnedest, ye blasted seas!" he roared. "Judique is on the floor, and who the hell will dare to put her off?"

This was enough to start Wild Archie, and all the rest of that battling breed into a whooping outburst. Little Roary the Piper could not withstand the inspiration of such a moment. Leaving his toiling watchmates on the deck, he went tumbling down into the sodden cabin to loosen his immortal soul upon the sheepskins.

"Ye can no tune yer pipes down there, can ye?" sang out the skipper.

"Aye, aye! I could tune 'em on the hinges o' hell at sic a moment," answered the piper, and soon the music of his drones came booming through the cabin skylight.

At the skirl of the pipes the Highland crew became like men possessed.

"We may be dead in a minute," sang out Red Alec, "but we're in our glory now."

Little Roary remained at his pipes, doing the work of twenty with his wonderful lungs of leather, for the witching strains of his screaming drones made every other man as good as two.

Shriller and louder the pipes skirled while every Hielanman leaped and whooped, accomplishing his tasks with rushing ecstasy. These Gaelic shipmates were aroused at last to the acme of conflict with waves and tempest. What mattered now Arch Campbell's shrieks of terror? Such coward tones were drowned by the gallant pibroch.

Suddenly over the skirl of the pipes came the cry of the man at the sounding.

"By the deep eight."

In the midst of broken water the racing schooner had found the current which ran like a river across the sandy shoals.

Following the trend marked out by the smoother surface Red
Alec threaded his way amid what from to seaward appeared like a
mammoth boiling caldron. Arch Campbell had prophesied that no
ship could live there, but the *Pass of Balmaha* raced merrily past
shoals and destruction, while the pipes of Little Roary shrieked
out defiance to the fiercest howlings of the sea.

When they were almost across the lookout screamed: "Luff!
Luff! Breakers ahead!"

Though his Hielan heart was aflame his hand maintained its
cunning, and Red Alec once again cheated death by inches. A few
more crowded, breathless minutes and the white water disappeared
on port and starboard and the Atlantic opened out before.

The skipper ran on, coming gradually into the lee of the island. There he ran into the wind and came to anchor with the
west point light bearing east-northeast on the point of rendezvous
for the fleet.

"What's the time below," he sang out as he left the wheel.

"One o'clock," came back the answer.

"Nine hours to the Western Bank!" said the skipper. "They'll
say we've cheated the sea, and by the leaping lightning so we have.
But we shan't tell 'em it was the music o' the pipes that done it."

The *Royal Stuart* leading the remainder of the fleet, after an
arduous beating to the windward arrived on her berth two hours
and a half after Red Alec.

Great was the amazement of Ronald Donn when he beheld
two lights instead of one. He expected the flash of the lighthouse,
but not the gleam of a schooner clubbed down at her riding
hawser.

"That can't be the *Pass of Balmaha?*" exclaimed the captain of the other vessel. "Surely that can't be her. She foundered on the other side of the bar."

As the *Royal Stuart* went ranging past her victorious rival, the unmistakable voice of Little Roary hailed him through the darkness yelling:

"Hey, there, Ronald Donn! Gang hame an' git another chart afore ye match yersel' wi' a skipper that kens his way to the Western Bank."

The Avenger

"Who killed your father?"

Shouting across from one schooner to another, "Ace" Bolce taunted "Wild Archie" with sardonic humor.

They had come together on the eastern end of Quero Bank. It was a fine morning. In the long and lazy roll of the Atlantic the two vessels bobbed up and down, like fine ladies curtsying to one another.

Outwardly, all things were propitious, but there was no curtsying on the part of the respective crews. Judique started to swear back as soon as the Hairleggers spoke to them with a cursing hail. To say that these crews hated each other would be to express it mildly.

The Judiquers had always claimed the title as champion fighters of the North Atlantic. This title went with them, whether they sailed out of Canso, Lunenburg, or Gloucester.

Their real challenge came with the accession of the Hair-leggers, a bunch of ocean gangsters, who were ostensibly out for the fishing, but virtually in the more precarious profession of rum running.

From the very beginning, Ace Bolce, king of the Hairleggers, had taken a violent antipathy to Wild Archie. Needless to say, his feelings were reciprocated. Between them it had been a case of hate at first sight.

Ace Bolce, the sly fox, was too sagacious ever to attempt an open fight with the giant. He was canny enough to bide his time.

Said he, "My specialty's knifin' 'em in the back. I'll get him yet, an' what's more, I'll get the whole bunch. Before I'm through I'll clean up that there MacEacheren gang, till there's nothin' left o' 'em, but the piece o' an ear an' a shin bone."

Wild Archie, as became a lion, did not descend to the level of blow and bluster. He was a dour Gael, of the hit-first-and-talk-afterward variety. He did, however, go so far as to growl.

"Ace Bolce's coffin's hangin' on the collar beams."

There were two hundred and eighty-five pounds of Wild Archie, and judging by the way he could kick the plaster out of a nine-foot ceiling, his growl bore something of the content of a death warrant.

Everybody allowed that Ace Bolce had bit off more than he could chew. But Ace was crafty. He matched the strength of the great, wide open, with all the viciousness of the city gangster.

Highlander and Hairlegger first fell foul of one another at Saint-Pierre, Miquelon, the rendezvous of those who were engaged at running cargoes of booze. To pay duty on such a necessity as strong liquor outraged the Highlanders' sense of independence. After the defeat of Bonnie Prince Charlie, it seemed to be more than ever incumbent upon them to rob the excise men of the King's shilling.

The Judique Jacobites came to the shores of Cape Breton with free trade in their veins. But do not let any one speak of their little pastime as common smuggling. For them, it was vastly more. It was a sporting proposition, full of risk and danger, where the clans of "auld Stuarts" still had a chance to chuck England under the chin.

The coming of the modern rum fleets soon blotted out the high-stepping game of the free trader. With the changing order it became a sordid, low-down, dirty business, where pelf supplanted pluck, where the sporting spirit vanished utterly.

Paddy Mack, one of the premier rum runners of the brave days, got so disgusted with conditions that he abandoned smuggling altogether, and went back to raising spuds.

All this conflict of the old order and the new came to a head when the Hairleggers fell foul of Judique. Between them it was an irrepressible conflict.

"Alexander of the Battles," sire of that fighting brood of MacEacherens, went to his grave lamenting.

"God only knows what we're comin' to, wi' the likes o' them sailin' out o' the Treaty Ports.

"It used to be fair fightin', and even odds, where best man wins. Now it's a case o' hijackin' an' pistols, where the damndest scoundrel comes out on top, and the finest man goes under.

"Aye, I'm glad I'm dyin'. Wi' the breed we got in the rum fleets these days, this world ain't fit to live in. We used to have lions and tigers in the woods, now we got nothin' but chipmunks."

Alexander died as the result of an encounter with Ace Bolce. No one saw the scrap. According to rumor they met in a dark alley of MacNair's, where the old man was found later with a fractured skull. The theory was that he had been blackjacked, and Ace Bolce was quick to claim the honor.

After the old man's death, Wild Archie, his son, followed after vengeance like a Holy Grail. The pride of his race, the honor of his clan, the love of his sire – these were the forces that urged him on – no slight forces in the fiery soul of a Celt.

On the night of his father's funeral, Wild Archie had done something that the outside world could hardly credit. He had given shelter to the alleged slayer of his sire, unwittingly thrust upon his shore by storm. Why had he extended this strange hospitality? Because, in Judique, "a stranger is a sacred name."

After that Ace Bolce had gone boasting up and down the coast, telling how Wild Archie was afraid of him.

"Didn't I say I'd clean up the bloody MacEacherens? There's Allan, an' the old man gone. With everybody scared o' that thing they call Wild Archie, didn't I go an' snap me fingers under his face, right there in his very home? Call him a fighter? He ain't got the spirit o' a louse. Jus' wait – I'll get him next."

In spite of all his bluster, Ace took good care to make himself scarce any time Wild Archie showed up. Ashore, he walked circumspectly.

But this morning when the rival schooners met out in the open seaway, it was a different story. Out here Ace felt secure, able to flaunt Judique to his heart's content.

The Highlanders would have rammed them, and climbed aboard for an old-time fight, but unfortunately the Hairleggers had the wind.

At the wheel of his own vessel, Ace luffed her up just enough to keep clear, yelling out a continuous rain of abuse.

"Ahoy there, ye Judique stiff. Think ye're the cock o' the walk, don't ye? Think ye're the finest scrapper that ever came down the pike. Well, when ye're sproutin' daisies, I'll still be kickin' my heels in the sunshine, an' dancin' wi' Tracadie women. If there's any wishin' in the grave, ye great big hulkin' stiff, ye'll wish ye'd never started mixin' wi' me!

"Who killed yer father – who killed yer father?"

This last fling set Wild Archie into a paroxysm. Beside himself with rage, he shouted back.

"Sling out yer dory there, an' come out an' meet me."

"I'll meet ye all right, when I'm good an' ready."

Wild Archie, goaded to desperation, started to cast off the gripes of his own dory, muttering.

"By jinks, I'll clean him up on his own vessel."

Throwing prudence to the winds, he would have taken this bold course, but the skipper called.

"Let that dory tackle alone, Archie."

"I'm goin' over there to fight him."

"Not while I'm skipper."

"Why?"

"Because, if you ever got there, they'd knife ye to ribbons."

Even in his rage, Wild Archie saw the skipper's reasoning. Hence he was forced to stand by in silence, while Ace Bolce kept up his flings, winding up with that incessant taunt about his father – and this, in the face of his own shipmates, was unbearable.

"Lead me to 'im! Oh, lead me to 'im!"

Wild Archie stamped up and down the deck, muttering a fervent prayer.

"Oh, Heaven, lead me to 'im!"

His bronzed, weather-beaten face had turned to ashen gray, his breath came in panting gasps.

Suddenly, in a frenzy, he ripped open his homespun shirt. Tattooed in China ink and gunpowder on the bared left breast appeared his own and his wife's initials, with a heart between, and the Saviour on the cross above.

On this most sacred symbol, the Judique giant placed his hand and swore a solemn vow of vengeance. Many a dour Highlander standing by backed up their champion in his vow.

That winter, Ace Bolce quit the sea, and went to join the shantymen on the Miramichi.

On hearing this Wild Archie also came ashore from the halibut fleet, and not even waiting for a trip home, started at once to walk four hundred miles to the north of New Brunswick, in order to come face to face with his foe.

He spent the whole winter on the drive, passing from one lumber camp to another. But Ace Bolce always eluded him.

In the springtime, Ace went back to the fleet with his old gang. Wild Archie went back likewise.

Sometimes their vessels spoke each other on the banks. But the Hairleggers seemed to take good care never to encounter Judique ashore, or in the outports.

Whenever his mates would commiserate with him on his long disappointment, Wild Archie would answer.

"I can wait – my time will come."

Early in the summer, with the first of the mackerel fleet in the Gut of Canso, MacNair's Cove began to be thronged with shipping.

In the midst of the Strait, a sort of ocean tollgate, MacNair's was the port where the feuds of the fishing fleets were settled. Because of its bellicose atmosphere, it was known as "the battle ground of the East." Here, among the hundreds of vessels passing through, there was a certainty that the Hairleggers would sooner or later appear. Here Wild Archie then stood on guard, watching every new topsail that came into view around the Sunnyside Bend.

There was something deadly in the way he was continually passing up and down the water front, like a wild beast on the scent of its prey.

As he passed, every one turned to watch him, exclaiming as he moved relentlessly on his way:

"That's Wild Archie!"

He was indeed worthy of a second glance. Cast in the large mold of the North, he handled himself as lightly as a kitten. Such blending of agility and strength carried with it a sudden sense of awe.

Stephen Graham, one of the old-timers, who had killed a bear with his naked fist, was forever croaking:

"Judique men ain't what they used to be."

But the old-timer cut out his croaking whenever he saw Wild Archie pass.

In the throng one afternoon Wild Archie fell in with that cherished trio, John Mystic, John Startling, and John Bluejacket. John MacDonalds all, Judique skippers out of Gloucester, differentiated by the names of vessels they commanded. For "auldt time's sake" the four of them repaired to "Black Denny's" rum shop.

In the rum shop, talk soon turned to the unsettled grudge.

"It's a cryin' shame, Archie, that we haven't been able to get that gillie. He's been shootin' his face all over the outports on the way he cleaned up the MacEacherens."

"Well, what about las' winter on the lumber drive on the Miramichi? I was followin' him all up an' down the river, but he was always jus' one jump ahead the fight. What's he got to say about that?"

"He don't tell about that. Indeed, we fellers from Gloucester never heard nothin' about it neither, till we blowed in to Black Denny's. We all thought that ye was playin' possum."

"My heavens, if I only could 'ave got at his throat, out there on the Banks that time."

"Yea, if ye could 'ave met him there, ye'd have soon finished the story. But he don't tell about that, Archie. He just tells about the way he flaunted ye to yer face in yer ain hame."

"Too bad a stranger's a sacred name up here in Judique," lamented John Bluejacket. "What wouldn't Wild Archie ha' done wi' him, if it hadn't a bin fer our folk's crazy theory o' hospitality."

"Nay, nay, ye canna talk that way. If the law o' the stranger didna go down North, then Judique wouldna be Judique," answered John Startling.

"Right and true," agreed John Mystic. "It's that kind o' Hielan honor, that when I'm far away, still makes me dowie for the auld land. Because o' that I'm proud o' Judique."

"Aye, aye," seconded John Startling. "God only made one breed o' Judique men, an' then He bust the mold."

"All o' which only makes it seem worse," complained John Bluejacket. "There's them Hairleggers makin' a laughin'stock o' the Hielan fleet all over the fishing banks. Twelve months gone, an' they're still makin' a holy show of us. Ha' ye heard the latest about 'em, Arch?"

"Nay, I ain't heard no news o' 'em for months."

"Well, I'll tell ye, after ye lads left fer home last fall, Ace Bolce an' his gang come ashore at Fox Island, an' attacked a shop kept by 'French Kate,' who'd just come there from the Tracadie. They stole everything, burnt the shop down an' would ha' kidnapped French Kate herself, if it hadn't been for a gang o' Gloucestermen. As it was, they allowed they'd done their damnedest just because they knowed French Kate was a sweetheart o' 'Red Alec.'

"Ace told her, 'Any one that's sweet on a guy from Judique'll get hell from me.'

"Then, the latest thing of all, a young feller from up this way named Roddie MacTavish, was in East River. Him an' the rest o' his crew goes into a dance hall on Cherry Street, and the Hairleggers happens to meet 'em there. When Ace got wise that MacTavish was from here he made a set on him, with his gang, an' in the fight one o' the Hairleggers chewed his ear off and nailed it on the door, yelling, 'That's what we do with ye, ye Judique pigs.' " The telling of this last affair raised Wild Archie to the supersaturation point of wrath.

"Get 'im!" were John Startling's last words as the party separated.

Because of his rage, Wild Archie's reply was slow and incoherent, but in the pauses between his words, it sounded to those who listened as if the bell of death were tolling.

For the following week the Judique champion had his spotters everywhere. He left no port or estuary unwatched from Glasgow Head to Sea Wolf Island. All his spotters rendered willing service as the eastern coast had suffered from the depredations of the Hairleggers, and all alike were yearning for the day of reckoning.

"At the first peek o' the brown sail, just slip me the word, and I'll be there, if I have to wade through fire and brimstone."

Of course, all this murderous intent could not be kept from the ear of Father MacDonald. On account of his vows of vengeance, Wild Archie very properly absented himself from the ministries of the church.

"I'll let me good wife attend to the prayin', while I take care o' the fightin'," he remarked. Consequently, he was not seen for many a Sabbath within the high, white walls of Stella Maris.

Father Donald, a fighting priest of a fighting parish, was not the kind to suffer long lapses on the part of his parishioners. The bishop had picked him because of other qualifications besides a degree of theology from Valladolid.

Returning from matins at the time that Wild Archie was hunting MacNair's, Kertsey, his wife, said:

"Father Donald told me he wants to see ye this evening, up at the glebe house."

Wild Archie's answer was shocking and irreverent.

"I ain't goin' near to Stella Maris until I've killed that there Ace Bolce. I don't care what kind o' curses they put on me. I tell ye I'm goin' to get this man before I'm through."

He left Kertsey, that good and devout soul, in tears and on her knees, and went out storming.

"I won't go near him, I tell ye!"

But outside in the night there were mystic forces. The darkness was full of awe, and from the high tower of Stella Maris the light was burning!

Every night, just after evensong, Father Donald placed that light in the belfry tower, to shine like a star on a wicked coast. Vessels beating in from the North Bay picked up that gleam, and their hearts warmed to their priest, who was wont to declare:

"My parish is the ocean."

Wild Archie stood there in the thick gloom, irresolute. Then, in spite of bluster, he went straight to the glebe house.

Jean MacEagh opened the door.

"Yea, Father Donald is in. He told me ye was comin'."

Old Jean ushered him into the study, lit dimly by the embers of a smoldering fire.

Over the fireplace was a large crucifix under which there hung a Ferrera blade, a Scottish broadsword that had tasted English blood at Culloden. This sword under the cross was the key to Father Donald – a man of faith and a man of fire.

The tall priest stood back in the afterglow. His shoulders belonged to the former champion hammer thrower of the Dominion, his eyes belonged to the man of God. He was a Keppoch MacDonald, sprung from a family of Jacobites of Lochaber, who had kicked out of the Highlands after the 'Forty-five. One of the lost-cause heroes of Bonnie Prince Charlie, this son of Keppoch had entered into the mystic heritage of the Gael, the heritage of a kingdom not of this modern world.

The wildest hearts in Judique were subdued in Father Donald's presence.

Without waiting for any preliminary, the priest went straight to the root of the trouble.

"Do I see murder in your heart, Archie MacEacheren?"

"Yea, Father."

"I know what it feels like, Archie. We belong to the sons of manly men. We come of a breed whose swords are ever ready, whose watchword is honor, whose lives are their chiefs'.

"The blood, the blood, it's aye the same. Back in the Hielan hills, and o'er the water here in Cape Breton Island, we're always fighting men. I know the call of the blood, Archie, and I won't tell ye not to fight, but I will say that ye must ask God to take murder out of your heart."

"I can't, Father." Wild Archie's voice was a cry of pain.

The priest did not answer. He withdrew, and stood gazing out upon the darkling mystery of George's Bay, while the crucifix and the Ferrera blade looked down upon that shadowy room, as on a sanctuary.

In that moment, Wild Archie was torn with conflicting emotions. The fitful, feverish hate of past months contrasted strangely with the serenity of this quiet study. Here, in a single flash, Father Donald had given him a glimpse of the white hills of truth, a flash of something above the base and sordid.

When, at last, he seemed to be in a better frame of mind, the priest came back to the fire and talked with him again.

"Why is it that you hate this man, Archie?"

"Ye ken that Father, without the askin'."

"Why?"

"Because he's made a laughin'stock o' Judique, because he's raised his dirty Hairlegging fist against our clan, an' still more because he's killed me ain father."

"Do you really know that?"

"I know, as sure as I know I'm here in Judique."

"Did you see him do the deed?"

"Nay."

"Did any one else see him?"

"Nay."

"Well, dinna tell me that ye know. And beware of hate, Archie, for hate breeds hate. It's the devil's ain sowing, the sowing of a wicked harvest. Pray for the strength of a man to be granted unto ye, Archie MacEacheren – pray for that noble strength – and leave the settlement to God. 'Vengeance is mine, I will repay, saith the Lord.'"

"Aye, an' that's what ye told me auld man before, Father Donald. Ye told him that very thing, an' now he's in his grave, an' Ace Bolce is livin' to make a mockery o' his name. Nay, I will na leave it. I'll do the job myself."

While Wild Archie was loud in his declaration of vengeance, the priest was quick to note a certain hesitation in his tone. He had seen the nobler course as well as the baser, and obviously was torn between the two.

Sensing that inner conflict, Father Donald knew that his arrow had found the mark. He was a man of few words. If the inner battle had been precipitated, that was enough. Without further parley he bid his visitor good night.

There were stirrings of something better in Wild Archie's heart as he passed out again under the shadow of Stella Maris.

For the first time in many a month he went back to the peace of his home, where the good Kertsey prayed in secret for him to be delivered from his awful passion.

That night he slept serene. But with the cold-gray light of dawn that murderous intent was there again.

For some time he sat in sullen silence, then suddenly he burst out of the house, exclaiming:

"I've got to get him!"

On that same day he returned to MacNair's, to watch the topsails of the north-bound fleet.

"No sign o' the Hairleggers?"

"No sign o' 'em yet," was the answer.

"Ye seem to be keen on that vessel," some one ventured.

"Nay, it ain't the vessel, an' it ain't her crew. There's jus' one I'm wantin'."

He was sitting in Black Denny's rum shop, utterly discouraged, when a number of Port Hood fishermen entered. They had just crossed the bay from the Outer Island, where they had been curing fish.

The Port Hood crowd opened up the conversation. Having been away fishing off the Magdalens, they were not aware of Wild Archie's quest.

In a casual remark, one of them said:

"The Hairleggers have come, so I s'pose we must all watch out. They're at the Outer Island at this very moment. They got some bait down the coast, an' I s'pose they're stealin' wood over there now. Anyway, we wasn't lookin' for no trouble, so we beat it."

Wild Archie appeared unmoved, but he rose and left the group precipitately. He went directly to the beach, shoved off in a dory, and rowed to a catboat, cast off her moorings, made sail, and set his course for the Outer Island.

Just off the lighthouse of the Outer Island, he signaled to his friend, Bill Rigg, the light keeper, to come out for him. Shortly after, Bill appeared in the lighthouse tender.

"'Ave ye seen anything o' a vessel wi' brown sails around here lately, Bill?"

"Yep, I seed a bloke like that lyin' off the nor'west point last night at sunset. I ain't been round to-day, but I s'pose he's there yet. Dunno whether it's a smuggler from Miquelon wi' rum, or jist a chap wot's waitin' ter stand inshore to cure 'is fish. I 'opes it's a smuggler, fer I ain't 'ad much since Red Alec, worse luck, went back ter the fishin'.

"I mind the time the *Vigilant* chased Red Alec in here, and what's he do but pitch his cargo overboard on a fishing trawl, one jug at a time, attached to the snoods of the trawl. Then he goes away and leaves the whole thing marked by a trawlin' buoy.

"When the *Vigilant* boarded in, Red Alec 'ad nothin' aboard but a few 'undred pounds o' salted fish. It was a joke after, to see 'im an' 'is crew apullin' up o' that there trawl, with the jugs o' rum bobbin' on the snoods. Course, I couldn't 'elp 'em, but it made me dry just to watch that kind o' fishin'. Well, come up to the lighthouse, Archie, an' ha' a smile."

"Naw, Bill, I got to look after this lad wi' the brown sail."

"All right, I'd go wi' ye, Arch, but I got to polish me lenses." Then he called after him, "If yer friend with the brown sail 'ave got something, don't ferget your old friend Bill."

"I'll look in again," answered Archie as he hit the trail into the bush.

"Seems in an uncommon, desp'rite hurry, he do," said Bill to himself.

Coming down on the opposite side, Wild Archie saw smoke curling from the shelter in the ravine. His heart gave a leap of joy.

"I've got 'im! I've got 'im!"

Coming up stealthily to the shelter, there was no sign of any one without.

"Something queer. Looks as if they been havin' a spree and they're sleepin' it off. That's bad. I'll have to wait to give him a chance to sober up afore he's able to put up his dukes."

While Wild Archie surmised that he might find the Hairleggers incapacitated through liquor, he did not, however, take any chances. To him one man in a fight against twenty did not appear alarming. He had tackled such odds before. But he was canny, as well as mighty, and he allowed no chance of ambush. He knew the nature of his foe, and realized that the gangsters would make short shift with him if they got the chance.

"To make sure, I'll jus' be takin' a look at the beach."

A moment later he came over the top of the bluff that commanded the northwest anchorage.

"Hello, no sign of the vessel in the offing – no sign of a dory on the beach. That's funny – the fire up on the shelter surely means that some one's there."

Coming back, he listened stealthily at the door. A low moan, as of some one in pain, came to his ears. Wild Archie opened the door and strolled in.

A bright blaze was burning merrily in the rough fireplace, while some abandoned creature lay huddled in a bed of spruce boughs in the far corner.

As Wild Archie stood in the doorway, the wretch looked up languidly. Then, as a slow perception stole across his dull senses, he exclaimed:

"Aye, it's you is it, you Judique pig. Well, you can't scare me this time, for all yer size. Kill me quick, that's all I ask, and put me out o' misery."

It was Ace Bolce who spoke from the heap of filthy rags – so pale of face, so sunken of eye, so deathly sick, that Wild Archie could hardly believe it was his mortal foe.

For a moment the big MacEacheren stood there in silence while a wave of pity swept him.

He could not bear to see even his vilest enemy in such a dismal wretchedness. As Wild Archie stood there his face underwent a strange transformation. The fighting aspect passed, and instead there shone from his eye the light of warm-pulsing sympathy.

"I came to pound the livin' hell out o' ye. If I'd a found ye in good health, I'd a broke every bone in yer Hairleggin' carcass. I'd a made a worse hash out o' ye than ye are now. But the hand o' God has done it for me. An' when I see what a mess the Almighty's gone and made o' ye, I say ye deserve it, but I'm sorry, seein' how dreesome ye're lookin'."

This pronouncement was met by an oath from the wretched Ace, who, though weak in body, had suffered no dimunition of his gorilla attributes.

"Well, it ain't for me to hit a man that's down, callin' names to ye again, seein' that yer so sair stricken. What can I get ye? Tell me that. But first, what ails ye?"

A spiteful gleam came into the eye of the gorilla as he answered.

"What ails me? I got somethin' that you'll get, too, for nosin' in here, an' stickin' yer ugly face around my deathbed.

"Stand there an' grin, but ye'll crack yer mug on the other side before yer through. I'm tellin' ye you're in a shanty what's bug house, jammed full o' sudden death, an' yer dose is comin', too, I got the smallpox!"

Wild Archie jumped back as though he had been hit between the eyes.

Smallpox! The very name was a terror of terrors to the big Highlander. He was bold enough to fight against any number, but there was something in the terror of this disease from which his highly superstitious nature shrank as from the power of darkness.

As a lad he had gone through a plague of smallpox, when many of the Judique fleet had died on Sea Wolf Island, amid scenes of abandoned horror that had haunted him ever since.

Without waiting for another word, he decamped at the double, and proceeded to put the width of the island between himself and the shanty.

On the opposite shore he found Bill Rigg busied at his chores.

"What ho! Ye're comin' back fast, ain't ye. Have ye found them blokes? Or is the constable after ye?"

"The vessel's gone, but I found the party I'd been lookin' for. He's got the smallpox in the shanty by the gulley."

"The 'ell 'e 'as! An' who might the bloke be?"

"It's Ace Bolce. I was just goin' over to kill him, but when I heard he had the smallpox I beat it fast."

"Beat it is right, Archie. Ye can't run too fast when ye're meetin' that kind o' plague."

"Yea, but now I'm over here, I can't help thinkin' that I oughtn't to leave him to suffer without a hand o' help."

"Bah! You should worry. What 'ave you got to do with all the blokes dumped on this forsaken island?"

"But I dinna like to think of any one being left alone."

"Let him rot, that's what I says. I believe in takin' care o' meself, first. If I'd a gone to every bloke abandoned here, I'd a been pushin' daisies long ago."

The cockney light-keeper made such a case for self-preservation that Wild Archie decided to give the dreaded island a wide berth.

"That's right – every bloke takes care o' his own self," agreed Bill, as he proceeded toward the tender.

This last remark jarred upon the Highlander. Such a philosophy was foreign to his every instinct, and he began to reason with himself as he walked toward the dinghy.

"If a stranger is a sacred name in our ain hame in Judique," he thought, "perhaps also it's a sacred name over here on the Outer Island. It would be awful to get the smallpox. But sure, it would be worse not to be good to a stranger."

Bill Rigg rowed him back to his catboat, talking all the way, but Wild Archie had fallen silent.

He encountered head winds on the return trip to the Judique shore. Long before he made port, the night had fallen. Then, out of the gloom, he picked up the gleam from the tower of Stella Maris.

"Aye, there's Father Donald, God bless him. He's gone an' lit the light again."

Instinctively, Wild Archie crossed himself, muttering half aloud one of the evening prayers of the Western Isles.

The lives of these Gaelic fishermen were steeped in the awe of the everlasting. Dwelling on "the true edge of the great world," praying was as natural to them as breathing. But many a month had gone by since Wild Archie had remembered his aves. To-night there was something in that light that called him back.

He was about to let go his head sheets and shoot up into the wind, when a familiar voice seemed to be speaking to him from behind the gleam of Stella Maris.

He hung on to his tiller atremble. For there in the darkness Father Donald himself stood gazing down upon him, the same merciful look in his eyes that he had seen on that last visit to the glebe-house study. But to-night the eyes of the good priest had something of reproach, as well as of mercy.

So real was the appearance that Wild Archie was starting to remonstrate.

"I had to leave him, Father! I had to leave him!" he was expostulating, when the apparition faded, and he saw again only the light from the high church tower.

But the light itself had become an accusing finger pointing him back to the Outer Isle.

Wild Archie was not seen again on the mainland for many a day. He cut himself off from the rest of the world, dwelling in that pest house, nursing and caring for his sick enemy. He cooked his food, tidied the shack, kept up the fire, and carefully watched over every need of the smallpox victim.

On his part, Ace Bolce remained the bitter dog. Without a single generous sentiment he continued reviling Wild Archie throughout his kindly service.

"Let me die in peace, can't youse Damn yer soul – why do ye want to plague me on the way to me grave? Get the 'ell out o' here, and let me kick the bucket without no show. Get out o' here and let me be. I don't want yer stickin' around here, I'm tellin' ye."

Then, in moments of diabolical hate, the gorilla would open up his taunting on the death of the elder MacEacheren.

"Who killed yer father?" he would sneer, while there in the candle light, the face of Wild Archie would become horrible with pent-up rage and passion.

The call of the blood was in his veins, the old strong call of the Highland hills – a call as strong as life itself was urging him to vengeance.

At such moments he could not trust himself to remain in the shack. Rushing into the night he would cry aloud:

"My God, my God, I must be at him yet!"

Out there under the trees, sometimes for hours, he would fight this battle with the beast. He could have torn the gorilla limb from limb. At thought of his father he could have ground him with his heel, and gnashed him with his teeth. Every instinct of blind rage urged him to smash and rip, gore and tear. And then in his wildest moments another power reached forth to hold him back.

Came a night when Ace Bolce was worse.

"I'm goin' to get a priest," said Wild Archie, feeling that the deathwatch was at hand.

Ace Bolce had been lying in apparent stupor, but with these words a kind of madness seized upon him. Rising on his elbow he began to revile Wild Archie with the most withering blasphemy. Seeming to gather strength from hell, he poured forth his torrent of abuse.

"It's bad enough for ye to lengthin' up me misery. But for ye I'd be already restin' easy in me grave. I tell ye, I don't want no priest around me while I'm passin' in me checks. I'm goin' to hell like a sport, and take me dose. I'm dyin' game, do ye get that?"

"Ye're a dyin man, an' that's enough for me. I'll be bringing Father Donald, for ye'll be needin' him to point ye to the guidin' lights."

Father Donald, at any hour of day or night, stood ready – a pilot for that last channel. All his life he had been braving seas and storms at the call of the dying along his far-flung parish.

When Wild Archie arrived at the glebe house, in the midst of a howling storm, as usual he found the priest in readiness. No inclemency of weather, no wildness of sea could hold back this son of Keppoch in holy orders.

That night he braved the Outer Bay in its wildest mood – fearlessly, and in an open dory. Wet and thoroughly chilled, he persisted to the other side, and passed on immediately to the shack of the dying man.

What transpired inside, in those last moments, was hidden from Wild Archie. He remained without, pacing up and down, watchful always.

Finally Father Donald emerged.

No word was spoken between them, but Wild Archie understood. For some moments the two remained by the door of the shack.

Then the priest's strong hand rested approvingly on Wild Archie's shoulder.

"And why were ye so bitter against him?"

"He killed my father."

"He did not."

"Ah, but I know he did."

"Nay, in his own confession he said Alexander MacEacheren had an attack there in the alley, before they ever came to grips."

"An' what of the fractured skull?"

"That was where he fell on the flagging. Out of sheer wantonness, Ace Bolce let you think all the time that he had done the deed."

Wild Archie's face suddenly went livid, as the meaning of this divulgence dawned upon him.

"An' to think I might ha' murdered him for nothin'!"

"But ye didn't. Ye did the better thing, instead."

"What was that?"

"Ye showed him the quality of mercy. How many times must I be telling ye, Archie MacEacheren, that mercy is a strong man's vengeance?"

Theodore Goodridge Roberts

Theodore Goodridge Roberts, the youngest brother of Charles G.D. Roberts, was born in 1877 at Fredericton, New Brunswick. After briefly attending the University of New Brunswick, he left school and eventually moved to New York, where he became the sub-editor of the *Independent*. In 1898, while serving as a correspondent in the Spanish-American War, he contracted malaria and was forced to return home to Fredericton. Following his recovery, he worked for more than two years in Newfoundland, editing the *Newfoundland Magazine* and working as a freelance writer. During this period he also sailed on a barquentine to the West Indies and South America. With the outbreak of war in 1914, he enlisted in the Twelfth Battalion. His distinguished war service included time spent as an aide-de-camp to General Sir Arthur Currie. Although Fredericton remained the centre of his life, Roberts travelled widely and lived with his family in many different places in Canada and abroad. Between 1900 and the late 1930s he wrote more than thirty books, including the sea novels *The Toll of the Tides*

(1912) — published in the U.S. as *The Harbor Master* (1913) — and *The Wasp* (1914). He was also a prolific contributor to magazines. His last years were spent at Digby, Nova Scotia, where he died in 1953. In recent years, Roberts' work has begun to be rediscovered. This long overdue attention has resulted in several anthology appearances and two important collections: *That Far River: Selected Poems of Theodore Goodridge Roberts* (1998), edited by Martin Ware, and *The Merriest Knight: The Collected Arthurian Tales of Theodore Goodridge Roberts* (2001), edited by Mike Ashley.

"The Flurry" was first published in *Maclean's Magazine* (March 1, 1930). It is one of many uncollected sea stories that Roberts contributed to various Canadian and American magazines. Like much of his maritime fiction and poetry, it testifies to the lasting influence of his short residence in Newfoundland and Labrador. It also typifies the humour that Roberts brought to much of his short fiction.

The Flurry

Cornelius Fitzgerald was the only native son of Pothook Cove who sailed blue water and foreign voyages. The others were content with the bay fishing, and a trip to "the ice" now and again in the spring of the year. And, come to think of it, Corney Fitzgerald was not what you might properly term a native son of Pothook Cove, for his father had been a Chancy Tickle man, and Corney himself had been born at Chancy Tickle and fetched north along into Pothook Cove when five years of age, by his widowed mother, who was a daughter of Andy Sprowl of the Cove.

Corney would never have been one of your ordinary outharbor noddies even if he had stuck to Pothook Cove and the bay fishing, for there was a mixture of wild blood in him from the Fitzgerald side; and from the mother's family — well, hadn't the first tilt in Pothook Cove been built by a runaway gunner's mate from a ten-gun brig, and hadn't that daring man marked all that coast with his name? Tom Sprowl's Cave, Tom's Head and Gunner's Head, Sprowl's Drook, Gunner's Barren.

When Corney was fifteen years old he worked his way around into Bonavista Bay and from there sailed on his first voyage, and he did not show his nose in Pothook Cove till four years later; and he was an able seaman then. He was soon off again, and after two more years of seafaring came home a boatswain. His mother was a proud woman. As for his grandfather, Andy Sprowl, he could not talk of anything but the grand naval family of Sprowl, and guns, and boatswains' pipes, and admirals – but his voice being weak from age and bawling for his dinner, nobody had to listen to him who didn't want to.

When Corney Fitzgerald came home the third time, he was Mister Fitzgerald, a navigator and second mate of a bark – with the papers to prove it right in his pocket. The bark was laid up in Harbor Grace for extensive repairs, and Corney enjoyed a prospect of six idle weeks. He came home in style from Harbor Grace to Rum Island Harbor in a fore-and-after, and the rest of the way in a hired "bully" – a chunky craft with a half-deck, handy and capacious. He arrived in February. He crossed the shore ice and the icy landwash with gloved but empty hands and his feet in goloshes and his head in a bowler hat and a cigar sticking from his jaw; and behind him came two lads from Rum Island Harbor with his seachest and nunny-bag and a lumpish object done up in a bit of red blanket.

The great man was Corney, sure enough, with a green parrot in a brass cage, a silver bracelet and a jar of guava jelly for his mother, and five pounds of tobacco for old Andy Sprowl. The widow was a proud woman, but old Andy was dead.

The folk of the Cove crowded into the widow Fitzgerald's tilt until the four walls bulged and the little windows threatened to fall out; so eager were they to see and hear the grand navigator at close quarters and maybe, try his goloshes and bowler hat on their own curious extremities. Among them were Mary Walsh and Willy Arkwright who were planning a wedding for next summer, weather and fish and luck permitting.

Boatswain Fitzgerald had not noticed Mary Walsh five years ago, for she had not been especially noticeable as a scarecrow girl of fourteen, but Mister Fitzgerald noticed her now. Being a blue-water man, he did not conceal the fact that he saw her and liked what he saw; and he grabbed back the silver bracelet from his mother – for hadn't she the parrot and the guava jelly? – and slipped it on to Mary's round left wrist. Then he gave the tobacco, that was now of no use to his grandfather, to Mary's father. Corney was a fast worker.

Willy Arkwright, the poor bay noddy, was distressed and angered by Corney's attentions to his girl; and the girl's reciprocal attentions affected him like a cold knife through his heart and hot ashes down the neck of his shirt. But being dull and ignorant and poor, what could he do about it but look like a fool? He was humble-minded, God knows! Who and what was he alongside the second mate of the bark *Good Luck*? What did he know of blue water and the great world of "up-along" who had never been farther from Pothook Cove than Fogo to the southward and Tilt Cove to the northward – never out of Notre Dame Bay? He had

long entertained a sneaking fear, deep in his heart, that Mary
Walsh was entirely too beautiful and desirable to be held for ever
by either himself or Pothook Cove. For a year now he had been
half expecting some trader to put in with a smart fore-and-after
and take her away from him; and here was Mister Cornelius Fitzgerald instead, in goloshes and a hard hat, with rings on his fingers
and conquest in his eye and his talk full of Pernambuco and
Oporto and Liverpool, flying fishes and waterspouts and hurri-
canes, and owners and captains crooking their elbows ashore to
the tune of "Down the hatch, Mister Fitzgerald!" – if hearing is
believing? And Willy believed every word of it.

Three weeks went by, very agreeably for Corney Fitzgerald and in
a confusing glitter for Mary Walsh, and with the torments of the
damned for poor Willy Arkwright. Willy tried to hide his suffering
but was not successful. He possessed no art of manner, no trick
of expression or conduct. As his temper was naturally mild, he
was able to refrain from violence; but beyond that, the best he
could do was to maintain a sulky silence. He sulked; and no one
loves a sulker. One may pity a sulker – but even that for only a little while. Mary, instead of feeling ashamed of herself, soon felt
ashamed of Willy – of the fact that she had been on friendly
terms with the sulky fellow. His own father and mother soon tired
of his sulks and lost their just sympathy for his sufferings. As for
Corney Fitzgerald he despised the sulking, spiritless noddy.

A lad named Waddy stole away up the cliff and on to the
barren one March morning at the first blink of dayshine, with his
father's sealing-gun in his hands and a craving for fresh meat in his

belly; and he looked abroad to seaward to the westward and northward, and shaded his eyes with a trembling hand, and looked
again, and let off the big gun with a roar that awoke the little harbor and a violence that knocked him flat on his back. But he was
up again in a second and scrambling down the cliff path, yelling,
"Swile! Swile!" at the top of his cracked voice.

The Greenland seals and Greenland ice were on the coast.
The seals in their hundreds and thousands had come close inshore
to deposit their young on thin ice. The wind was on the shore.
The heavy arctic floe crushed along the "whelping-ice" – and
there, on the thick ice and the thin, rode old hoods and harps,
square-flippers and bedlamers and new-born whitecoats. It was a
harvest that could not be neglected. Every able-bodied man and
woman and youngster of Pothook Cove took part in the garner-
ing. The women and youngsters and stiff-jointed old men worked
on the nearer seals, the old men batting the poor innocents over
the head with their gaffs and depriving them of hides and coats
of blubber with their "sculping knives," and the women and
youngsters towing the blubbery hides ashore. The lively men went
farther; and the liveliest went farthest of all, killing and killing, on
and on, leaving the "sculping" and towing to the less lively and
venturous.

Willy Arkwright was a master in every department of that
blubbery business. At swinging the gaff, at handling the knife and
peeling the white fat off the thin red flesh, and at running broken
ice he had not met his match in five years. Now he went through
the ranks of the inshore whitecoats like the Angel of Destruction,

leaving the sculping and towing of his kill to his followers. He passed beyond, seaward, on to the hummocky Greenland floe, and fell upon big yearlings and square-flippers and the parents of the herds like an avenging god. Here he did his own sculping, and "panned" the heavy skins of blubber and hairy hide on a rocky knob that stuck up clear of the crowding ice a long sea mile off Pothook Cove. He thought he was all alone; and then his nose caught a whiff of burning tobacco, and he looked up and over his shoulder from the job in hand at the moment; and there stood Corney Fitzgerald, grinning at him from under the brim of his hard black hat and smoking a cigar. And that was not all of it. Corney wore his fine gloves and grand black overcoat, like a merchant from Harbor Grace, and those goloshes on his feet. Then Willy Arkwright stood up and turned around, and all his rage and self-pity fumed up from his heart and melted his tongue, and he told the sailor what he thought of him and how he felt about him.

Corney did not say a word till Willy was through, but flipped the grey ash off his cigar and kept on grinning. Then: "Maybe ye didn't notice the wind's shifted round an' blowin' off shore, Willy b'y," he remarked.

Willy's rage went up into his brains at that. He cursed all the winds of heaven, and defied winds and ice and sea to stop him batting and sculping before he was ready to stop; and then he cursed the blue-water sailor all over again; and finally, spurred to the crowning absurdity by his maddening fury, he dared Corney to stay right with him till he was through with the seals.

"I be wid ye, b'y," accepted Corney cheerfully.

Willy Arkwright returned to work. It was not a great while before the tow to the knob of rock became too long to be practical; so Willy began a new cache of skins on the ice itself. Corney went away out of the desperate sealer's sight among the ice hummocks two or three times in the course of the next two hours, but did not remain away over ten or fifteen minutes at a time. Not once did he raise a hand to help Willy at killing or sculping or towing; and not another word did he say about the wind – not when it took to circling and became white with snowflakes, even.

At last, chilling fear got the better of Willy's insane anger, and his nerve broke. He flung his wet knife away and screamed at Corney that the floe was adrift, and that they could not be discovered in the blinding "flurry" even if boats put out in search of them, and that they were the same as dead already.

"Ye speak trut', b'y," agreed Corney. "If ye be done wid yer foolishness, I'll take ye ashore. I got a rodney beached on the ice t'other side dat hummock."

Willy's relief was so great that he laughed and wept. They rounded the hummock of blue ice. The rodney was not there – nor was the section of flat ice upon which the sailor had berthed it. Under the actions of wind and rising seas, the floe had cracked and parted between the rodney and the two men. Willy collapsed at Corney's feet. Corney stared to seaward, and through a rift in the twirling flurry glimpsed the detached pan and the little boat not more than thirty yards away to leeward. So he kicked Willy with his grand goloshes and told him to get up and swim. But Willy could not swim. True to the tradition of his kind, Willy Arkwright had never learned to swim.

"Git up an' git in, anyhow, an' I'll float ye acrost," said Corney. "It bain't over t'irty yards."

Willy looked at the dark water and said he would sooner die on the ice. Corney begged him to move, explaining that he could not win across to safety with more than his own weight if the distance increased by more than ten yards, and that the channel was widening fast. Willy replied that he would sooner die on the ice than be drowned. Then, without another word, Corney removed his overcoat and goloshes and Willy's outer coat. Willy protested; and Corney picked up the gaff and batted the stubborn bay noddy over the head as neatly as any seal was ever batted, then heaved the unconscious form into the icy sea and plunged after it.

Corney made the distance, with dumb Willy in tow – but ten yards farther would have been too far. The unconscious noddy wore a knitted scarf around his neck; and that was lucky for him, for without it Corney could not have kept him afloat while he hoisted himself out on to the ice. Corney was a fast worker. He launched the rodney, dragged helpless Willy aboard, and pulled dead in the wind's eye back to the starting point of his short but chilly swim. There he got into his dry overcoat and goloshes and buttoned Willy's dry coat about Willy's heavy shoulders; and from there he struck shoreward across the floe, pushing the rodney before him like a sledge with Willy in it. He was a strong man, but he needed all his strength then. He was a brave man, but he needed all his courage in that struggle against wind and whirling snow, breaking ice and rising sea. And he had yet another cause for worry. Had he batted poor Willy a mite too hard, maybe?

The floe was breaking into a score of big pans, into a hundred smaller pans. Corney came to the splashing edge of ice,

launched the little rodney again and manned the short oars. The
wind was whirling, but he sensed the general drift of it and pulled
steadily for the hidden shore until he bumped ice. Again he took
to the ice and sledded on his way, and again he launched on to the
rising seas, and yet again he mounted the ice. He reached the lee
of the cliff which he could not see because of the twirling veils
of the flurry. Here he rested long enough to pluck a flask of red
rum from his hip, pour a few ounces of it between Willy's teeth,
and rub a dash of it on to his own ears. Willy let a moan out of
him, which lightened Corney's heart.

The flurry was abating somewhat when Corney reached the widow
Fitzgerald's door with his strong right arm supporting Willy Arkwright. His mother screamed with joy at the sight of him, but she
couldn't get a word about the desperate adventure out of him until
he had put Willy to bed in warm blankets and poured a mug of
hot tea into him.

"Gulch her down, Willy b'y," he encouraged. "Ye bain't dead
yet. I'll sweeten the nex' wid a snatch o' rum, b'y."

His mother told him that he had better be giving a care to
herself, all but prostrated with anxiety as she had been, and her
widowed heart still flapping with the shock of his return from the
clutches of death, instead of nursing Willy Arkwright like his own
baby; and the neighbors, who had come crowding at word of the
lost sealers' arrival, agreed with her. Mary Walsh was there, in ab-
solute agreement with Mrs. Fitzgerald.

"Why wouldn't I be nursin' him like me own babby?" retorted Corney. "Wouldn't he be dead now but for me – froze to deat'
on the ice?"

He continued, with words and manner now arrogant and now persuasive, to tell them that Willy Arkwright was a man to be proud of – the bravest man he ever saw, save only for a natural fear of deep, cold water – and the stubbornest. He had often heard tell, he said, of determined persons who would cut off their noses to spite their faces, but he had never believed it possible of human nature until he had seen Willy do it, in a manner of speaking. Had not Willy kept right on batting and sculping to seaward just for spite, knowing all the while the ice was drifting off shore and carrying him to sure death? Aye, he had that! It was different with himself out there, with a rodney beached on the floe to paddle back to shore in – but Willy had been as ignorant of the rodney as any squid.

Most of the listeners were simply bewildered by his talk. Mary Walsh was amazed and shocked. Only Willy, there in the warm bed, approved of it.

Corney talked to Mary alone later that day, in the lee of Dave Walsh's tilt, holding her tight by a round wrist most of the time.

"Bein' wed to a blue-water sailor bain't no life for a sweet, bewitchin' lass like yerself – but when I see the spite o' Willy Arkwright out on the floe, willin' to drift to hell hisself so's to take me wid him, I took a horror of himself an' Pothook Cove too; an' didn't I square me account wid Willy by savin' his life an' maybe his mortal soul – and maybe 'twouldn't be no worse for a lass to be lonesome ashore i' Harbor Grace six mont's togedder."

He released her wrist then and embraced her slender body with both arms.

They sailed out of Pothook Cove seven days later in Tony Webb's bully, and were married at Fogo.

Willy Arkwright still brags about the brave, stubborn man he is —
for did not Corney Fitzgerald give him the name of it? — and he is
happy and consequential all day long telling how he traded his girl
for his dear life, handing her over to a blue-water sailor in return
for being floated across from one pan of ice to another — and
himself that tired of the girl he was glad to be rid of her. Which
suggests that the stroke of the gaff delivered by Mr. Fitzgerald on
that noddy's skull was even a better and more merciful thing than
he had intended at the moment of striking.

Further Reading

Regrettably, most of the sea-related writing by the authors associated with the Seaward School remains out of print. In fact, as noted in the introduction, much of it has never even appeared in book form. However, during the past three decades a number of maritime works by these writers have been republished. The following list identifies the titles that are currently available:

General

John Bell, ed.

Atlantic Sea Stories (Lawrencetown Beach, NS: Pottersfield Press, 1995). [Collects sea stories by the seven authors represented in *Against the Raging Sea*, plus fiction by W. Albert Hickman, Frank Parker Day, and Erle R. Spencer. Also includes an introductory essay, bio-bibliographical headnotes, and suggestions for further reading.]

Individual Authors

Frank Parker Day

Rockbound (Toronto: University of Toronto Press, 1989), with an afterword by Gwendolyn Davies.

Norman Duncan

Battles Royal Down North (Freeport, NY: Books for Libraries Press, 1970), with an appreciation by Wilfred T. Grenfell.*

Harbor Tales Down North (Freeport, NY: Books for Libraries Press, 1970), with an appreciation by Wilfred T. Grenfell.

Selected Stories of Norman Duncan (Ottawa: University of Ottawa Press, 1988), edited and with an introduction by John Coldwell Adams.

Way of the Sea (Ottawa: Tecumseh Press, 1982), with an introduction and bibliography by John Coldwell Adams.

Wilfred T. Grenfell

Adrift on an Ice Pan (St. John's: Creative Publishers, 1992), with an introduction by Ronald Rompkey.

The Best of Wilfred T. Grenfell (Hantsport, NS: Lancelot Press, 1990), edited and with an introduction by William Pope.

Down North on the Labrador (Freeport, NY: Books for Libraries Press, 1970).

Labrador Days: Tales of the Sea Toilers (Freeport, NY: Books for Libraries Press, 1971).

Off the Rocks (Freeport, NY: Books for Libraries Press, 1970).

W. Albert Hickman

Canadian Nights (Freeport, NY: Books for Libraries Press, 1971).

The Sacrifice of the Shannon (Halifax: Formac Pubishing, 2001), with an introduction by Ian Johnson.

Colin McKay

Windjammers and Bluenose Sailors (Lockeport, NS: Roseway Publishing, 1993), edited and with introductory essays by Lewis Jackson and Ian McKay.

Archibald MacMechan

At the Harbour Mouth (Porters Lake, NS: Pottersfield Press, 1988), edited and with an introduction by John Bell.

Erle R. Spencer

Yo-Ho-Ho! (St. John's: Creative Publishers, 1986), with an introduction by Ronald Rompkey.

Frederick William Wallace

Under Sail in the Last of the Clippers (Glasgow: Brown, Son & Ferguson, 1986).

* The Books for Libraries Press reprint editions noted above can be obtained from Ayer Company Publishers (Suite B-213, 300 Bedford Street, Manchester, NH, USA 03101. Tel: 1-888-267-7323. Email: ayerpub@yahoo.com. Web site www.ayerpub.com).